Where's My Wine Glass?!

Getting Your Kid to College Without Losing Your Mind

LINDA PRESTO

Where's My Wine Glass?!

Getting Your Kid to College Without Losing Your Mind

LINDA PRESTO

woodhall press

Woodhall Press | Norwalk, CT

Woodhall Press, 81 Old Saugatuck Road, Norwalk, CT 06855
WoodhallPress.com

Cover design: Jessica Dionne
Layout artist: LJ Mucci

Library of Congress Cataloging-in-Publication Data available

ISBN 978-1-954907-52-2   (paper: alk paper)
ISBN 978-1-954907-53-9   (electronic)

First Edition
Distributed by Independent Publishers Group
(800) 888-4741

Printed in the United States of America

This is a work of creative nonfiction. All of the events in this memoir are true to the best of the author's memory. Some names and identifying features have been changed to protect the identity of certain parties. Names, characters, places, and incidents either are the product of the author's imagination or are used fictitiously. Any resemblances to actual persons, living or dead, events, or locales is entirely coincidental. The author in no way represents any company, corporation, or brand, mentioned herein. The views expressed in this memoir are solely those of the author.

For my mother.
Thanks for the funny.

Contents

vii

ONE

Applications and Fabrications

Somewhere around September of each year, the phone numbers from panicked parents flash on my business line, each saying, "Pick up! Pick up! I need help!" Parents just like you want to set up a time when I can come to their home and sit next to their fledgling child to be certain he or she completes and submits college applications. After doing this job for more than a decade, I understand: Students don't want their parents glaring over their shoulder, squinting their eyes at the screen and critiquing every word they type. Likewise, parents don't trust their children to do this properly (or maybe do it at all) on their own. Applying to college has become a crazy stress test of parental indoctrination. The process involves all the touchpoints of successful parenting with the looming fear that should you fail, your response to other parents will be, "Yes, my kid still lives at home and works at the Chuck E. Cheese."

1

Applying to college properly is important and parents feel that pressure maybe more than their kids. As parents, we see what's coming, or, to be more exact, we see what they're screwing up as they're screwing it up when they don't have a clue. It's a clairvoyance I could do without, personally. So, each autumn as the leaves begin to turn their multicolored hues and drop with the temperatures, I sit at dining room tables across northern New Jersey and Zoom calls around the world to help students complete the actions that will lead to their college placement and help parents regain the ability to breathe.

Maybe when you applied to college it was a straightforward process of forms, manila envelopes, and a few stamps. For me, the hardest part was printing neatly on the designated lines and remembering not to put tiny hearts when I dotted my i's. Today, this process is more like a triathlon of organizational skills, focus, and carefully worded braggadocio. In addition to the several letters of recommendation, a few personal essays, a host of short-answer questions, some transcripts, and a test score or two, prospective students now need to submit a résumé to colleges and universities—a résumé! —from a 17-year-old who just last week farted so loud he posted it on social media to brag.

Honestly, what can these kids put on a résumé? The babysitting gig they had for the bratty kids next door, which they didn't keep because wiping snot just isn't worth the money? Yet, many colleges require these premature biographies for acceptance. It has become part of the insanity of this process, straining to create an impressive, inspiring experience from a six-week stint as a camp counselor at Barry's Horse Farm.

When it comes to résumés (and many other things), some parents develop a hands-off policy. I've had parents who only emerge from their hiding spots to pay me and revert to whatever idyllic haven they have constructed for themselves. I often wonder what they're doing in there: I envision some reading quietly, while others perhaps put on headphones and jam out to 80s classic rock. Truthfully, I have no idea unless they share, which some do: "I was eating chocolate in my closet," was probably the best response.

Another favorite of mine is parents who yell. I know that sounds counter to what seems proper, but the ones who yell are often releasing some of the pressure that builds up during this time. If their yelling isn't coupled with throwing harsh words or dishware, I think those families will make it through. I have been present for many an argument, and some people even pull me into their family disputes: "Tell him, Linda, shouldn't he audition for the choir *and* the band and send in an art portfolio? Isn't it *all* really important?!" Although I have learned the art of compromise (unless you ask my partner, I suppose), these are never easy situations, but they are commonplace. Parents everywhere are hating their children during the later high school years.

Maybe it's part of the cycle of letting go of them. Although, not to burst anyone's bubble, they rarely just go without returning home often, with their new, more substantial problems . . . and their mountains of laundry.

Perhaps the biggest difference between applying to college today versus in the dark ages when I did it is the use of technology. Sometime around the incorporation of my college coaching business, the online application was born. As we all know, applying to college online led to the **Common Application** and other applications intended to streamline the process. This online tool provides the ability to apply to all the colleges at once, if they accept the Common App. Some colleges are still holding out and don't take the Common App, like they're expecting technology to suddenly reverse? For those schools, you would apply directly on their website. So I recommend saving all the pertinent information in a separate document and copying and pasting as needed. Because students now apply to an average of nine or ten schools, the bigger dilemma is choosing the appropriate ones, much like selecting a toothpaste from the myriad choices on the shelf that all seem to tout "the whitest teeth!" or "the healthiest gums!" Like now we must worry about what our gums look like, too?

The process of applying to college is like having forty-one open tabs on your computer as well as in your brain, none of which is functioning properly. Technology has simplified the application process in some ways, but, in turn, it opened the door to applying to many more colleges, answering many more questions, and writing many more essays. (Another section will tackle the personal essay, because that task is like an exorcism of a very hostile demon, and he deserves his own rant.)

Trying to decide which colleges to apply to gets more complicated every year. Acceptance to college in the United States today is a sort of an enigma, and it can be as frustrating as solving a Rubik's cube. I have never completed more than three sides of solid color on that ridiculous box: It's a litmus test of concentration. Acceptance rates to the **Ivy League** schools have dropped from the low double digits to single-digit percentages, some even under 5 percent since the days of COVID. That's less than your chances of getting struck by lightning! For the math geeks out there, I am aware that the chance of getting hit by lightning in the United States is one in seven hundred thousand people each year, while there's a one in two thousand chance of getting into Harvard. So my comparison is more hyperbolic, but basically, getting into the Ivies is the equivalent of winning the Powerball. Only it's way more work.

While we are talking about Harvard, if you haven't been living under a rock the last few years, you are aware that some parents of a certain wealth and stature have paid (read: bribed) school officials to acquire a spot for their children at one of those top schools. It's a Netflix movie now, but it's been a practice for a while, sadly. Some parents think that because the über-wealthy and celebrities are willing to risk criminal prosecution to get their kids into one of these schools, well, they must really be exceptional schools. Here's my take: The most selective schools are usually academically challenging schools offering a stellar education and great opportunity, that is true, but they aren't for every student, and they aren't the deciding factor in being successful. And . . . you don't want to bribe people; it's bad karma. The best goal is one that includes a college that represents the best fit for each student, not the highest-ranked school for every student.

My daughter Jess wanted to attend a college for vocal performance. Talk about selective; Julliard wanted a professional portfolio and a produced and marketed CD. *If she had that, why the hell would she need to go to Julliard!?* I thought. **Conservatories**, like Julliard, are the Ivies of the music world, and similarly nearly impossible to get into. Eventually, after making mountains of chocolate chip cookies (I bake when I'm nervous), we found a university that offered a standard college experience but included an on-campus conservatory, where music was king, but you didn't have to be Lady Gaga to get in. It

Match Schools: Your transcript mirrors that of the average freshman at these schools. Your GPA, SAT/ACT scores, and course selection (AP, IB, honors . . .) will be comparable with those who have been admitted. This will not guarantee acceptance, because extracurricular activities, essays, and other items matter. However, you can apply with some degree of confidence knowing you have a good chance of getting in.

Reach Schools: These schools are colleges where your academic qualifications are below the average accepted student. When considering a reach school, it's still important to be realistic. If your test scores

5

was a place where Jess could learn and grow as an artist. Thankfully she was accepted to this school—the Hartt School music conservatory at the University of Hartford in Connecticut—for a wonderful experience and a degree in music performance that will not help her get a job at all. But that will be another book.

I don't know why those celebrity parents risked jail time to get their kid into any school, quite honestly. I am not going to jail so my kid can party at a frat house with the next Zuckerberg. Besides, Jess would not have thrived at Julliard, and we both knew it. The demands and competitive nature of some schools are too much for certain students. I have had students who had a good shot at being accepted into an Ivy and have chosen not to apply because the fit wasn't right. The pressure might be too much, and their mental health is important. We want our kids to flourish in college not break down. My nephew could have applied to a university at that level, but when his parents spoke with him about that, he balked, "Ma, those kids are

and grades are close but not quite there, give it a shot; an admissions staffer might just see potential or feel your personality and work ethic are a good enough fit.

Safety Schools: Pick at least one of these. A safety school is one in which your academic credentials exceed those of the average accepted student. For example, you have a 3.9 GPA and most of their incoming freshmen have 3.5, or you scored 1450 on your SAT (congrats on that by the way!) and most of their incoming class averaged 1300. With situations like these, there is a high probability that you will be admitted but not a guarantee.

too stressed out. I'm not going there." And he's not wrong. Getting accepted to an Ivy or other very prestigious school feels wonderful initially, but the important question is whether the student can thrive there. It's like making the cheerleading team but then finding out practice is every day and games are every weekend, and you thought it was just going to be wearing cute skorts and waving pom-poms when boys were around. That was me, and they should have made that clearer is all I'm sayin'.

Thankfully there are a multitude of colleges and universities to apply to in the United States! You're probably wondering, "Is that a good thing?" Well, it is often a good thing, but not if you've ever tried to help a student whose major is "Undecided" narrow their list of schools down from 104. I had a student once, let's call him Dave. Dave loved everything; he was the most pleasant damn kid you would ever meet. I loved Dave. Everyone loved Dave. Dave thought science was cool, history created meaning, English provided communication. Everything fascinated Dave. It may sound like a wonderful working situation, but, in fact, it was a hair-pulling event. Do you like city schools or country schools? "They're both cool," said Dave. "Would you prefer a large or small class size? "I could do either!" Dave exclaimed. Dave met every inquiry with excitement rather than trepidation. *How will we ever narrow down the selection*? I wondered.

I return to toothpaste. I try to choose a toothpaste in those fluorescent-lit, superstore aisles with bright-blue boxes with twinkly stars on them guaranteeing to whiten and shine, and another brand in green neon that's "tough on tartar!" But with so many choices, I think, how's a conscientious brusher to choose? It was the same for Dave with every colorful brochure or website he saw, promising the ultimate college experience in a neatly manicured landscape. Dave visited several schools with his parents, and then together we scoured the sites of hundreds more, hunting for reasons to eliminate them: "This one has a hard-to-pronounce name." "No, too many flowers."

"Those are crappy school colors." Anything that set them apart. Finally, Dave got his list down to twenty-one schools. Still sound like a lot? You bet! But somewhat normal by today's standards.

Both times I attended college, I applied to only two schools, and I had a tough time choosing. Today our kids are so terrified of not getting in *anywhere* that they're applying *everywhere*, creating all-time low acceptance rates due to an all-time high application rate. Essentially the competition of getting into college is perpetuated by those who are desperate to get into college. I don't discourage them, though, because—well, first, I'm not paying the application fees this time ... woohoo! But also, the likelihood is that they won't get into all the schools to which they apply. It's probable they will get into some; none of us knows which ones. So casting a net that is slightly wider makes sense if you're able to do so or you can get the colleges to grant you a free application (never hurts to ask!). Dave got into all except his reach schools; those are the schools kids apply to but know, based on their qualifications and the school's record of acceptance, their chances of getting in are slim. Dave's success in getting into many yet not his reach schools is still impressive, because it's not always the case. So many students don't get accepted to many of the schools they apply to like Dave did, but as I've mentioned, Dave is the nicest damn kid you'll ever meet. He would have been happy almost anywhere.

As I say often to kids like Dave and their parents, the thing about the process of applying to college is that it *is* important. No one wants to mess it up, not even the lazy kids. Everyone wants this to go well. I see students bite their nails and shake their legs under the table while their parents go through the slew of items on their to-do list. Sometimes I ask for a cup of tea or a glass of water just to get the parent out of the room. I was that parent; I get it. I could not get out of my way long enough to let my "young adult" figure it out. Because many parents like me think, *What if they don't?* Based on teenage behavior, this is a valid fear. The thing is, usually kids do figure it out when they do it on their own. And, yes, I know how irritating and frightening that can be. But resist the urge to do these college prep activities for them. Step away from the process as often as you can. Otherwise you'll end up in a dramatic episode of "Where did I go wrong?!"—a lovely little show where the protagonist (that's you) doubts every decision made and throws his or her hands up with a flourish while drinking wine. It might be an Emmy-worthy translation of the frustrated parent, but I have never met a kid who becomes more productive as a result.

I once had a mom tell her daughter, a senior at the time, that her grades were so crappy that she would never get into *any* of her choice colleges, so she shouldn't even bother. Yikes. Another parent wanted three essays and the full application done in my one-hour session. Um, probably not. There are a lot of expectations out there . . . and many of them are wrong. What you *can* expect is a busy fall in your child's senior year of high school; a very tense and stressful one if you have not begun the process early. The earlier you begin, the better it will be for your sanity, but no matter what, the fall of senior year is a scene from a bad B-list movie where the aliens take over and everyone is pretty much doomed.

Anything else is up to how you navigate this unruly ship and your child's personal feelings about it, which is the "perfect storm" up ahead. Get a life jacket.

Another confusing element of this process is the application itself, which should be a simple form with boxes to be filled in with minimal-word answers and dates of things your kid can't remember. These days, since the Common Application and some other coalitions like the University of California (UC) on the West Coast are accepted by most colleges, the process is simplified by the one-stop-shopping approach to applying. You fill out one application, and all schools receive the same information. Halleluiah! It's like going to those outlet malls where they have all the stores in one place AND chocolate from Godiva! Genius!

The application itself isn't difficult and only needs to be filled in once for all the colleges applied to, which is another reason kids apply to so many. It's a straightforward form with the information you'd expect to be asked:

- student and family profiles
- education information
- activities list
- the writing sections

That last one is the kicker. Each school has different requirements for writing samples from students; some are lengthy and require a great deal of time, thought, and effort. Luckily, teenagers hate all those things, and those who begin applying with a list of thirty-eight colleges end up with about eight or fewer out of sheer laziness and avoidance of those schools that want too much.

The Common Application requires one essay of up to 650 words, but most colleges request additional writing assignments of their choosing in addition to the main essay. The college essay(s) and questions are by far the most harrowing part of the process for most students and their parents. Who would have thought that a simple personal essay could cause so much strife? Yet, it does in nearly every single home, including my own. If the intention is to have students complete their applications in any kind of a timely manner or without personal and family angst, then the writing element is clearly the Achilles heel of the process; ironically, most students don't remember who Achilles was or what his foot has to do with anything.

There are other defects in this process as well. As stated, the entire application process takes place early in senior year of high school—a full year before students will be going anywhere. How many students do you know who can plan ahead three hours, no less twelve months? I remember my daughter seemed so overwhelmed by the process that

I finally asked her: "Are you *sure* you're ready to go to college?" Jess is a bright girl who had a fairly good idea what she wanted to do: study music performance. Believe me, that's specific; most students have no clue what they're even interested in, no less what job they might want to do someday. Jess wanted all those beautiful dreams people told her about, including me, but at seventeen she couldn't picture them from her uncomfortable high school desk-chair combo. (Who invented those terrible chairs?!)

When I asked her if she was ready, she said, "I think I will be, but I'm studying for a chemistry test tonight and have choir practice all day Saturday."

I realized kids can't picture what everyone wants them to see. They simply don't have a point of reference for it. College was once the place where students went to learn and figure out what they like and where their interests lie. These days by the time they enter senior year of high school, they're expected to know their major, a suitable minor, a possible honors program, extracurricular clubs and/or activities they'll do in college, and what job they want when they graduate. It's a little lofty if you ask me.

A lot of changes happened for Jess over the course of her senior year, and she did apply to music programs. As you know from the beginning of this section, she got into a school that had what she was looking for and was, in fact, ready when the time came, but senior year was not the chill time it used to be, not for her or many others. The biggest problem most of us had during our senior year was staying awake in history class or having our parents find out if we didn't show up to gym class all week. Maybe that last one was just me and my aversion to sweat-laden high school mats and any activity requiring coordination, which is why I am a writer.

Obviously, applying to college today is a multistep process of researching, without being too giddy like Dave; organizing your thoughts as well as your choices into categories; writing; editing;

begging; crying; negotiating; and, perhaps, drinking and/or praying, depending on what suits you. It also requires the proper timing, like it was for Jess—eventually. But is anyone ever hugely successful with a multistep process the whole way through? At some point the plan gets messed up: The teacher who promised a glowing letter of recommendation leaves the district, the guidance counselor holds the student's transcript hostage because he can't decipher the student's scribbled handwriting, or the scores for the SAT test your child took for the twelfth time a month ago aren't back yet. Then, after all the planning and struggling, comes the waiting, and Tom Petty had it right, "The waiting is the hardest part."

Takeaways

1. Your kid needs a résumé even if there's nothing to put on it.

2. The application process is banana pants.

3. Rich people might pay for access, and they might go to jail; don't be like rich people.

4. The "fit" is the goal, even if it doesn't impress your neighbors; who likes them anyway?

5. Narrowing down the list is hard if you have a "Dave."

6. Practice narrowing exercises while shopping for toothpaste.

7. Some parents yell, some eat chocolate in the closet; it's all okay.

8. Teens cannot picture their futures, and have no idea what they're doing.

9. Let your kid do some of this on their own, even though number 8 is true.

10. Eat snacks in the closet as needed.

TWO

Making the College List and Checking It Obsessively

With most things in life and work, and much to the chagrin of my own children, I have a system for everything. I think as humans we each get some useless gifts in our DNA; process is mine. Clearly, I did not hit the gene pool lottery. Developing processes is not glamorous or impressive or inspirational or even fun, but it does come in handy, and I have made a career out of it. You, too, can take your neuroses and make it your life's work—but that's a different book.

For now, let's focus on the monumental task of getting your child into and off to college, and the organized and effective way to go about it! No, that part isn't the joke, but the funny thing about making your college list, as with pretty much everything else in this process, is it is more about *who* your kid is than *what* he or she has done. For real.

I'm sure I'm compromising your opinion of my taste in music, but there's a song from the 1980s about searching that pops into my head every time I work with a student who is beginning to search for colleges and has no idea where to start. "The search is over; you were with me all the while . . ." Yes, it's old. Yes, the band members had big hair and looked better in makeup than I did. Yes, they wore jackets with shoulder pads and vests and suspenders—it was a weird time. The point is they were singing about searching for something only to find that the answer was already with them the entire time. Okay, they were singing about a tall, blond model in the video, but the idea remains: The answer isn't in books or based on IQ or dependent upon teacher recommendations. The song relates to not just pretty models but loftier ideas and ideals.

For instance, somewhere around junior year of high school some people—okay, mostly everyone—will ask you or your kid where he or she plans to or hopes to go to college. You will grow to hate those people.

"Have you started looking at colleges yet? It'll be here before you know it!" Ah, those well-meaning friends and family. They have no idea. They tell you, "I remember when I was looking at colleges for my Jimmy . . ." They ramble on as your eyes glaze over like the doughnut you wish you were eating. As their mind rescinds to last month or year, you are left with the anxiety of knowing you really haven't done much of anything in the way of searching for *your* Jimmy yet. You don't even know what "searching for colleges" means, nor do you have a "Jimmy." Worse yet, are the parents of kids who have completed this part of the process already. They will tell you about their college experiences like they are sharing war stories or childbirth nightmares, leaving you terrified.

I think the idea of "searching for colleges" is the equivalent of finding a new doctor: You know they're out there, hundreds—no, thousands—of them. You ask your friends and surf the net, read reviews, but it's difficult to know if you're going to like the health care provider until you go for a visit and he or she avoids eye contact or calls you by the wrong name. Or, if you're a woman, he tells you to "relax, it's just in your head." You want to be angry at him, but he also prescribed you some much-needed sleeping aids, so you go with it and move on to the next one on the list.

With that same uncertainty, colleges and universities will employ fabulous marketing and virtual tours, but it's hard to know whether each should make "the list." Perhaps your child has tried narrowing it down, but she has no idea what her major is going to be nor whether she wants a big school in the city or small school in rural America. Most children are startlingly little help in planning their futures. So parents usually begin for them on the computer, staring at the screen for a while, Googling "best American colleges" or "safest colleges and universities." Some may even refine their searches a little more, "colleges in northern New Jersey" or "colleges that offer degrees in zoology," just to see what they get. Likely the result will be in the millions, which doesn't make much sense, because we know there are not over three million colleges in New Jersey nor are there millions of universities that offer zoology as a major (trust me on that one). Internet searches are less accurate than they are anxiety-producing. If you simply search a more general "colleges and universities," then 3,999,000,000 results magically appear in 1.6 seconds, followed by a wave of nausea. This search session is clearly over.

Now you have officially begun the search; you just don't know what you're searching for. The first step is to narrow down this ocean of choices into a lake, then a pond, then a puddle.

No one can make sense of that much information, unless you're that guy from the game show, *The Chase*. The host asks him questions like, "In 300 BC, what animal was worshipped like a god by which group of settlers?" He smiles calmly and answers, "That's the turkey; turkeys were heralded as god-like creatures by the Mayans at the time,

15

and they were taught domestic roles in society." I'm not sure what happened in history since then, but if people then had turkeys helping with the housework, I can't imagine why my dog isn't vacuuming my living room right now. For us nonsavants, the process is the key to figuring out where our kid will go to college (and, if we're lucky, may lead us back to the days of animal housework!).

Students tend to begin their college search either poking around on their phones or clicking on a college ad on their laptop. Usually, though, they click on a site offering to help them "find the right college" and end up filling out a questionnaire asking everything from dorm preferences to shoe size and getting bored halfway through. Personally, I have always believed they should match up dorm roommates by shoe size. That's double the shoes for each of them! I can't think of anything more appealing. Plus, when they are half asleep (possibly hung over), they will have the right sized shoes on, so they won't fall off their feet! But it's likely they won't match or be on the correct foot. Who cares, they basically wear pajamas to class these days anyhow.

Other than getting sidetracked and overwhelmed, many students have difficulty with the "how" part of college searching. It can cause the initial procrastination that students experience, and parents respond to with panic. I've found starting a search with a few simple items is helpful. Here are three important things you or your child can look for first in your online search to help you breeze through the many colleges and reduce the number of possibilities (as well as your brewing migraine):

1. Mission/Vision statements

2. College news page(s)

3. Your specific program/area of interest, if known

If you methodically tackle these three elements for each college you look at, you will know relatively quickly if the school is one your kid might be interested in applying to. Do this, and you will save yourself a lot of time (as well as aspirin).

Sometimes the hardest part about the search is finding the darn mission or vision statement on the school's website. For reasons I will never understand, colleges and universities tend to hide the thing. Someone (likely an underappreciated writer like me) worked hard to come up with those words that describe exactly what the school prides itself on and what it hopes to accomplish; this statement is integral to the school's purpose. And it can be a hidden gem—if you can locate it!

Slogging through endless screens lit up with photos of cathedral doors, arched windows, and vast courtyards is entertaining for a time. The marketing writing in playful fonts displaying catchphrases like, "Imagine the Possibilities . . . " and parents and their subjectable children do! Or my local community college's: "Start here. Go anywhere." It's all very U.S. Army–like propaganda: "We Want YOU!" But do they, though? Parents watch the cute videos of the students and faculty and try to picture their own children in that environment. Inevitably, their thoughts are plagued with worry about the kids getting mugged under the orange fall foliage or behind the historical, but what looks to be very poorly lit Science Building.

Along with catastrophizing, parents are simultaneously annoyed with their children for not doing the searching themselves, and they usually storm over at some point in the process to tell them so. This scenario is one way searching turns to shaming, shouting, or sometimes shushing. Like my student Brad. Brad didn't know where to begin with his college search, so he didn't. Brad's caring and involved parents thought it best to do it for him, which can be a fine way to jump-start the process for avoiders, procrastinators, and others who mostly just play video games; I call them the "game-awayers." These are the kids who will do anything rather than peruse the colleges they might attend and live at soon—one of the great mysteries of our time.

So, if you're a parent doing your kid's online college searching, usually it's good to start with the "Home" or "About Us" pages and look there for mission and vision statements and other important information. Sometimes the statements are on a "History" tab, too. Especially the older schools tend to put their mission in with the information of how they came to be whatever type of college they are today. Histories are worth reading for information on the colleges, too. Although I've met very few students who care much if Ulysses S. Grant came through the campus when it was a horse trail.

Once you finally locate the mission and/or vision statements, you get a sense of the school's idea about itself. Who wants a college that doesn't know itself—so 1980s. Let me explain that a bit. Colleges and universities do try to be well-rounded in what they provide to students in terms of a stellar education, clubs and extracurriculars, and a safe environment; however, they each have specialties. Again, like doctors, some colleges are better in certain areas of teaching or have specific programs. So their mission and vision can give you a peek into what they hold most dear. For instance, some colleges pride themselves on their position in the community. University of Rochester is a good example. They have a specialty in music with the Eastman School of Music's renowned program, but they speak most about their place in the community. The staff there seem to relish the idea of holding events on campus or volunteering at community events off-site, always present as a part of the community in which they are housed. If community involvement is something that's important to you and your kid, too, then you'd know this school might be a good match.

Also, check the news pages on every school site you visit. It's surprising how much you'll learn about a school from what they consider news. For my athletically challenged children, the news pages with five articles about the football team and two more about the mascot made it clear this was a sports-centered university—great for those students who want to partake or watch or try for athletic scholarships, but not as much of a fit for my slightly spastic, yet otherwise gifted children. Though Jess would have enjoyed being part of Ohio State's infamous marching band, the size of that school would have given her hives from the first day. Think about what you would want on your family news page: "Young adult breaks record for most hours slept in a row." "Dinner is overrated—I'm making pie!" Whatever the highlights of your news pages, they are unique to you and your family, just as each college's will be to their school and purpose. Mine would definitely include pie.

The third stop on the virtual university tour from your bed is the area of interest. What's your child's intended major? Or possible major? Or major this week? It doesn't matter if he or she doesn't know, which is very likely. Sometimes looking at the specific curriculum can help a student decide. I've had countless students tell me they are going to major in business—until I show them the curriculum for that major at their selected schools. "I have to take how many math classes to graduate?" "Wait, what's engineering again?" These questions help me streamline the process of guiding them in choosing a major or deciding to go "undeclared," which is also fine for some students. Many spend freshman year at college figuring out what major they might like to pursue. Usually it comes down to which classes they liked best in high school or had the professors who were easy graders.

You want a school that is the best possible fit for your kid, not necessarily the best ranked school in the country. I know, this goes against the grain of popular logic these days, but if your kid doesn't feel at home at college, it's going to be a very... long... four... years. For all of you.

They likely won't do as well, and it's possible they won't stay. A feeling of belonging is fundamental to our human needs. Books have been written attesting to belonging determining the outcome of a student's success at school. As parents, we were reminded of this need for inclusivity every time we threw a birthday party. "No, I'm not inviting Suzie; she's a jerk!" "Yes, she's a jerk, but you still have to invite her." Or, "Don't forget to invite Sal!" "Who's Sal?" you ask. "He's my new friend." Followed by you silently wondering, *Is Sal real or imaginary?* Either way, you order the kid some pizza and hope he doesn't disappear.

TAKEAWAYS

- Lists are good even when they start with 132 schools.

- Finding the right college is more about who your kid is than what he or she wants, which is good because most don't know what they want anyway.

- Check mission/vision statement, news pages, and your kid's preferred major curriculum, to likely convince them they don't actually want that major.

- The search isn't over until the teenager sings (its college praises).

- It's okay if your kid is undecided; it's difficult getting information out of kids. Teenagers would make great prisoners in enemy territory; they say nothing.

- Let them have imaginary friends if it helps.

THREE

Planes, Trains, and Pasta Stations

Somewhere around Jess's entrance into high school, I realized neither of my children had ever seen a college campus. I suddenly felt like such a loser as a parent. The kids and I traveled all over the East Coast when they were young, visiting museums, live performances, plays, concerts, and shows of all kinds, but somehow we didn't stop at a college. She and her brother Ryan were young, and the thought of stopping at a university to walk around admiring old buildings and floral landscapes while pondering several years into the future was definitely *not* on their itinerary (or mine).

When Jess was in her sophomore year of high school, though, all the parents began talking about college visits: "Have you seen Moravian?"

"Yes, have you been to Michigan yet?"

"No, but this weekend we will be visiting Lehigh, Muhlenberg, and Penn State."

"How lovely, winter break we will be touring Wesleyan, UNC, and Coastal Carolina . . ." It was a constant barrage of college critiques and trip advisories. Parents all around me were taking their emotionally ill-prepared kids on planes, trains, and automobile trips all over the country to see where their future paychecks, **529 Plans**, retirement savings, and any expendable cash for the next several years would soon be going.

I had been working with high school kids as a tutor and coach for only a few years at that point but had insider information on how these trips were often not successful or fun. Mine, of course, would have to be different. I thought, *I should know what to do, I help students get into college after all!* But one thing I have learned over the years is that no matter what we adults are good at, our children seem to want no part in it. No matter how much we know, to our children we don't know much. So, against my own better judgment, I planned our first trip to Ohio.

This trip was not to Ohio's capital city of Columbus or even their sort-of city Dayton, but the city of Oberlin (total population of 8,256). It's true, Oberlin isn't known for anything other than its university, unless you count its famous history of the process of reducing aluminum from its fluoride salts by electrolysis; the aluminum production invention birthplace, that's where we were. In fairness, we were there because Oberlin is a prestigious and selective college and music conservatory whose acceptance rate remains under 30 percent even today. Oberlin is one of those college towns where the college *is* the town. Jess, however, did not seem to mind this fact.

Knowing the music makers oversaw the town seemed to give her great joy. And I see her point there.

Oberlin is set up sort of like Disneyland . . . only creepier. There are rows of perfectly straight and clean storefronts, all seemingly freshly painted. Their historic buildings display an old architecture and have curb appeal, updated for an aesthetically pleasing look.

Their downtown eateries also have that old town feel resembling old-fashioned American neighborhoods from the early 1900s, lovely two-story historic buildings with wide concrete sidewalks in front so clean you could eat off them, though I wouldn't recommend it in these days of wanton viruses. The strips of stores were dotted with a five-and-dime shop and a hardware store instead of a Home Depot. The college is interspersed through the city, like many urban universities, but Oberlin is so beautifully picturesque it looks almost fake.

Walking down the streets, I thought we were in a *Truman Show* set; I was waiting to hit the ending picture of the horizon. When we drove a few blocks past the college, it was as rural as 1700s American heartland. I thought that would be the sparsest surroundings we would see in visiting college towns, but . . . I was wrong. Many universities have an area of exurbs circling them, yet some have *absolutely nothing*.

The following month we visited Susquehanna University in Susquehanna, Pennsylvania, technically named Susquehanna Depot, a name that screams, "We are not progressive!" The university was pretty and academically sound, but leaving the university looked like we had landed on the moon—vast amounts of land with dirt flooring. In addition to the locations and surroundings, I was trying to ascertain if these schools could provide the education my kid needed and not simply a row of sororities and beer-pong parties. To be certain we were getting all the information our tired brains could manage: We went on the obligatory "campus tour." I guess it makes sense to see the campuses with someone who knows where everything is, but it felt a lot like we were on a sloth's journey through old structures and pedestrian crossings. It's like you're being held in slow-motion captivity so they can sell you everything from upgraded dorm rooms to a new pasta station in the cafeteria (that pasta station was outstanding, by the way).

I wondered at times if Jess was taking any of this tour in as information, or if she was simply mentally decorating her dorm room and planning her next meal as we walked endlessly through the campus and town. She did perk up at the site of Warner Concert Hall, the location used for student and faculty recitals. Then I knew for sure she was mentally shopping in her head for the perfect dress for her own recitals. The tours are designed to show students and their parents (and the unlucky siblings along for the ride, like my son Ryan) many areas of the college to sort of picture themselves in the environment. Or to learn they can't.

The tour, like many others, took us through the cafeteria, where I recommend eating while you're there, and lecture halls. They pointed out lovely landscaping and their best dorms that only the seniors get; they don't usually show you the freshman dorms, because often those look like abandoned psychiatric hospitals from the 1950s. In addition to the tour, there are lectures, meet-n-greets, PowerPoint presentations, and motivational speakers available throughout the day and into the evening.

Despite your willingness as a parent to give up large blocks of your ever-fleeting time, somehow your kids often do not enjoy this experience. They mope and shrug at every question. Anything you like, they make faces at. It's like they revert to their seven-year-old selves being carted around in a grocery store against their will. I'm all for deciphering passive-aggressive behavior, but this entire excursion is *for* them, so their reaction quickly becomes maddening to parents, understandably. Apparently, they have not noticed that their parents want to be there even less than they do. As parents, we are looking at every penny of disposable income and savings going to this clump of lecture halls and dormitories, and we won't even be there to enjoy the damn pasta station! We go home with nothing but a T-shirt and a copy of a **FERPA** form. The stress and general aversion to growing up seems to cause acute anxiety and an apparent immaturity that makes you want to leave them at the cheapest college you find and go the hell home.

While my brother and sister-in-law were visiting colleges with my nephew, they arrived at their third stop of the weekend, and my nephew refused to get out of the car. They had driven four hours to reach Villanova University, and my nephew looked out the window for a millisecond and declared, "Nah, I'm not going to go here." These young creatures are insane. I don't think they can help it. They're like the pod people from *Invasion of the Body Snatchers*, empty vessels of annoyance wandering around without blinking. It is important for students to get a feel for the college, and sometimes they will realize it's not the right place for them, but they could get out of the car and allow a leg stretch at least. My brother said (I'm assuming as calmly as possible), "Get out of the damn car and look at the college you will not be attending before I run you over!"

I had a student once who refused to go and see colleges at all, which I guess is better than getting there and not getting out of the car, but only in the money saved on gas. Her poor parents were beside themselves, imploring her to look at the colleges they had so diligently chosen for her. Eventually she did go to her local university, slogged around, and then took a gap year. Not that a gap year is a terrible choice; for some, it's the best choice. But after taking the time to visit colleges, it's not an exciting ending. I can't help but wonder if kids derive some sort of pleasure watching their parents squirm. Perhaps it's a last hoorah of childlike manipulation before they go. Whatever it is, I can promise you, you will not miss it when they are gone.

Thankfully there are tour guides at colleges–nice young people whom you did not raise, therefore they don't hate you. College guides are the happiest people on Earth. They must be the leftovers from the Disney applicants. They always smile and gush about their college. They are the most active students on campus, joining several clubs, sports, and extracurricular activities. They are the glee club members and the a capella group participants. And they are the same people who hold the "Welcome" party for the freshmen, who no one else even notices on campus until they're crying in a corner because they can't find Dewey Hall. The tour guides make parents feel like maybe their kid will be okay and smiling too, until they realize guides get paid to lure your children, which makes you feel like you were just bamboozled by Pennywise the Clown.

That frightening thought brings us to the next important element of the college visit: the campus security department or campus police. These are different at every school, so it is worth checking with each college individually, but basically these are the people who are entrusted with the job of keeping your child safe while they are on campus. They will *all* look unqualified to parents.

Some campus police in some state schools can have statewide authority and jurisdiction that is similarly afforded to the state police. Others are comprised of Jimmy the Pothead and Larry, the security guy from the mall. It's worth a visit while you're there to see which they are. Not to mention, most colleges will tell you how safe their school is, but you will be able to see which ones keep bars on their windows. In seriousness, though, this is an important stop on your tour. Find out where the building and the officers are, when they are open, and how to contact them if needed. Plus, when you're catastrophizing because your kid hasn't answered your text in the four seconds since you sent it, you will have faces to go with the nightmare.

Other areas to consider exploring are the student spaces, where they hang out and do homework or post on social media. These are the places they will be when they aren't hiding in their rooms or falling asleep in class. These areas also allow visiting kids a chance to get a feel for the students at the college. They are trying to picture themselves in the acrylic purple chairs of geometric shapes (I don't know how students ever get comfortable in school). Meanwhile, most parents don't even realize that's furniture. Sometimes kids will catch a glance of someone at a table who gives them a half smile and, for a second, they feel less like a guest and more like a potential student.

If the half smile comes from someone cute, there's a good shot that school will make the list. It's a terrible reason, I'm aware, but at this point you won't care anymore.

The other thing to think about, while your kid is going gaga over someone on a tie-dye beanbag chair, is making an appointment with a member of the faculty, preferably in the department that your child is likely to major in, if you are lucky enough to know that. I looked up the department head for music management while visiting colleges with my son Ryan. At Hofstra University we had a campus tour and then were offered sandwiches in a room filled with round tables. I was getting my much-earned sandwich when I bumped into Will Stevens, the guy in charge of the music management program there at the time. I introduced him to Ryan, and the two instantly hit it off. They talked for more than an hour about bands, touring, ticket prices, "merch," and other things I could not comprehend. Meanwhile, I ate my sandwich by myself. But when applications were reviewed, I was fairly certain Ryan would be in good shape. And he was. He got in and ultimately decided to attend Hofstra University, so of course Mr. Stevens left the school a year later. Of course, he did. But Ryan received some valuable information about the coursework and the program that he might not have otherwise known. Admissions cannot always answer specific questions about a particular major or program, so try to get in front of someone who can. Nowadays, these meetings can be done virtually as well.

All these things will help, but there are no guarantees of an acceptance even after a good visit or meeting. Take notes and talk to as many people as you can. Track down professors and pop in on the folks in financial aid; there's a good chance you'll be speaking with those people often (unless you have enough to bribe the college officials instead). I was on a first-name basis with Donna at Hofstra for four years. She told me which grants and loans to apply for and how, as well as which scholarships were available that I would not have otherwise known about. Think of it like visiting a friend and applying for a job at the same time. It's a friendly bunch of people, and it's good to enjoy yourself, but what's the salary and are you going to get three weeks' vacation are the important questions.

Oftentimes it works out fine. The students tend to like the schools that like them, and visiting at least gives them an opportunity to be likeable. And to leave you alone eating a sandwich.

Top 10 Things to Know About COLLEGE VISITS

1. Do them. When possible, tour colleges of interest. It will give you and your kid a lot of information about the school and a feel for how far your kid will be from the cafeteria.

2. Be prepared. Bring questions to ask and take notes, because you won't remember, and your kid won't care enough about the important things to take note.

3. Drag all your children along. I know that sounds terrible, but it amounts to fewer visits and less you'll need to do for the next kid.

4. Note size, location, campus/city atmosphere, as well as what's *around* the university too. You'll want to picture where your kid is hanging out; it makes the moments of worry and panic much more specific and visual.

5. Visit campus security! Oh, yeah, be *that* parent. You can find a wealth of important information from the folks who keep the kids safe; most of it you won't really want to know, but some is necessary.

6. Grill that paid college tour host! But not so far you make him or her cry. Don't be a monster.

7. See the dorms but *do not* have high expectations. Do not look at those Facebook posts and fancy rooms the college seniors have. Most freshmen dorms are equal to the summer camp plywood boxes we stayed in when we were young. Closets, they were basically closets.

8. Interview with someone from the specific program or major of interest while you are there, if possible. Also, speak with the students you meet while on campus. Ask them what they like best about the school and what they would like to see changed or fixed. You might obtain valuable information, or you might get nonsense about a tough professor who refused to give credit for a paper they handed in two weeks late. It's a crap shoot.

9. Locate the health center so your kid knows where to go should he or she get sick or have an injury. Meet the staff and allay some of your fears—well, hopefully.

10. Eat at the dining hall while you are there. Also, visit student spaces and the bookstore, classrooms, and lecture halls. The more your child sees, the more he or she can ascertain if it feels like a good fit.

11. Oh, and tell your kid ahead of time that getting out of the car is mandatory. (Yes, I know, that's eleven. I'm not much of a rule follower, even when the rules are my own.)

FOUR

What Do These People Want?!

A lot of students ask me this question in relation to college admissions boards. Parents ask it twice as much, if not more. Everyone wants to know *who* to be and *how* to be to get into that coveted college. My answer may not be what you think. Of course there are standard criteria most colleges look for while deciding on prospective students. It's fun to listen to parents picture the admissions staff as "overworked, overtired sloth-like creatures slogging through essays," or as "powerful chameleons who smile at you while you're there and then send your application into oblivion when you are gone." It's logical to me that parents would think of them this way; these people have incredible power over your child's future. Since I have seen them in captivity, I'm sure admissions counselors are just regular people. For parents, though, their influence and judgment will have a direct effect on the next four years and perhaps beyond. I had an epiphany about that

31

when my kids were applying: I think it's the fear that if your kid can't build a successful future, then his or her dirty socks will always be on your floor.

Most parents and students stress over these criteria for a long time before they even begin the applications, but no one criterion holds the needed element or carries the most weight. There are a lot of myths and misinformation about the admissions process. One is, "You should totally name drop for the college you want." Well, in my opinion, unless it's someone close to you, it's just going to sound weird. Like, if your grandfather was an alum, great to mention that, but you should probably not talk about the celebrity who attended that university that you met for fifteen seconds; then it's just awkward.

Another misconception I hear often: "The more activities I have done, the better it looks." No, it doesn't. It could end up looking like, "Maybe this kid has too much nervous energy to burn and voted most likely to set your car on fire." Or my personal favorite myth: "Colleges look for well-rounded students." No, I don't think so. I believe they want a well-rounded student body; understanding that difference might just change your outlook on the entire process. And it might help you to not want to drink an entire bottle of wine in one sitting. Not that there's anything wrong with that.

What I have witnessed is that students do not need to have years of volunteer service, nor do they need a perfect GPA. Elements other than grades and volunteerism are important to colleges when they make selections. (That and how much drinking the counselors have done before reading the apps. I'm kidding, of course, but who knows? It might be true.) They include the following:

Grades. Of course every university looks at a student's grades. Grades are the source of much (perhaps most) of the angst in applying to college, but it's not necessarily as simple as a one-number GPA above 4.0. For those who are unaware, I'm sorry but the numbers do go higher than 4.0. No wonder it stresses everyone out. Some students with AP classes, IB classes, or another accelerated program can develop a GPA above 4.0. My advice about grades is similar to how I feel about weight and body image for young people: If they keep moving the goal post, then don't bother chasing it. When I was young, which after 2020 feels like it was another solar system in a faraway galaxy, girls were supposed to be cute and pretty but did not have to be eight feet tall and emaciated to be considered model-like. As I got older, I realized that no matter which crazy diet I tried, I was never going to look like the girls in *Cosmopolitan* magazine, never. I found this revelation to be quite a relief. If I couldn't reach the goal, then I was free to eat pizza and Doritos without guilt. Much the same (perhaps twisted) mentality goes for grades. The powers that be continue to raise the standards of what top grades are, so basic is best; if you can get your kid to do the best *he or she* can, then you're on the right track.

Grades are important because they encompass a great deal of information about the applicant. A perfect line of straight A's down the transcript is not needed, but having one tells the counselors something more about how this student operates. Effort and improvement weigh heavily as well. So, if your kid had a C- in English freshman year of high school, don't bite off all your nails assuming his or her college career is over. Raising that grade shows colleges that your kid struggled and learned from that struggle and figured out how to improve his or her performance. Or he or she cheated much more effectively as time went on.

Class selection. The type and level of classes throughout high school matter a great deal to prospective colleges. This is only bad if you have one of those kids who refuses to challenge him- or herself. I had one of those. Ryan was (and still is) brilliant but lazy. Watching him spend ten minutes on homework and get a B+ when you knew another ten would have earned him the A was absolutely maddening. But parents know all children are different, and sometimes they get some bad genes (from the other side of the family, of course). Hopefully, the student is willing to challenge him- or herself and choose classes at the highest level possible. You want the class that will push your kid forward, not over the edge. However, I would be remiss if I didn't add that Ryan is also the least stressed person I know, so it's possible he's on to something.

Standardized test scores. Colleges are requesting test scores at varying degrees, especially since COVID, but some want them to evaluate how prepared students are to handle the type of work that college will entail. That's the terrifying part. To me, though, these tests mostly measure one aspect of students' abilities: how well they handle stress and the pressure to perform. If that's the case, they should just let them sing a song in front of judges or something. If they don't throw up, they're probably ready for college.

Allow me to repeat myself . . .

Admissions staff are regular people, not zombies of the apocalypse incognito. They have a bit of power, so think of it like a trip to the DMV or a call to the IRS: It's not going to be enjoyable, but you will likely leave with what you need.

Grades and class selection do matter; lazy kids beware!

Have your kids take the standardized tests, but don't bet the house on them; I'm not sure if that's a poker term, but what I mean is, if you had to put money on your kid's score, start low.

Activities are great, but your kid does not need

Extracurricular activities. This is the insane running list of every sport or musical instrument your kid has ever tried. Every time a student pulls out the "Activities List," I picture one of those old scrolls in a Shakespearean comedy that unravels down and across the stage. This is a situation of quality over quantity. Which activities did they pursue long-term? For which ones did they obtain a leadership role? What matters to this kid? That's all you need. One of those can go a lot further than a never-ending list.

Application essays and questions. Of course, this book has an entire chapter devoted to "The Dreaded Essay," but it's worth mentioning briefly here, because I have seen kids take a college off their list based solely on how much additional writing was needed to apply. When your kid says, "I don't know, I just think the Online School of Podiatry is a better fit for me than Chicago University," you are being lied to, my friend. I thought you should know, but honestly, it's understandable if you don't care.

to include the three-month stint playing clarinet and the sixteen different soccer teams he or she played with.

Positivism is annoying, but teenagers need some to help them seem less like, well, teenagers.

35

Letters of recommendation. Some students dismiss this one because they think they have little involvement in it. However, choosing the right teacher/coach/mentor to write a letter might be the most crucial part of this adult-and-child interactive stress test. The person or people your kid chooses for this task should know him or her well. I don't recommend choosing a teacher he or she just met in September of senior year; this person has no idea by October who your student is. If your kid's teacher is like me, he or she probably isn't even 100 percent sure of your kid's name at that point. This person will not know enough to deliver a powerful letter or impress the admissions staff.

All this information is nice, and I'm sure some or most of it sounds familiar, but the only real advice I would give is in a word: character. Determining what colleges think of you should involve your kid showing his or her true colors.

Character is how we react to life when something happens that we didn't expect. Have you ever taken a plane trip with someone whose character is lacking? It's like flying the catastrophic skies: [dramatically throws up hands] "I knew this would never work out! I knew something would go wrong." "Now what am I going to do? I guess that's the end of that, now we will be here until tomorrow! Or longer—oh, my God!" Meanwhile, I'm the person slurping the last of my Starbucks mocha-decaf-extra-whipped-cream-add-a-shot-to-help-me-sleep latte wondering if I can get two more because we're going to be here for a while. This is one aspect of character, and all areas of character take time to build—to evolve—so asking kids anything at this age is sort of strange to me, but here we are. The funny thing about character, though, is that even when we can't name specifically what it is, instinctively we know when it's lacking. So does the admissions staff. Your kid needs to be real. This reminds me of that quote: "Be yourself. Everyone else is taken."

Finding the right college is as much an inside job as it is a constant list of things to do on the outside. While you're busy making to-do lists for your kid and figuring out if a school has the right number of students and an acceptance rate that doesn't make you want to cry, they need to be thinking inward. Judging from their inability to disconnect from their phones for more than forty seconds, I'm guessing very few are having these moral and ethical moments of growth in high school.

What's their vision for themselves? Don't you hate when people ask the question, "So, where do you see yourself in five years?" Ugh, I have shuddered at that inquiry myself on job interviews. But what that question is really asking is, "What's your vision for yourself?" It's not about having it all mapped out to depict who you will be or what you will be doing, but rather what's your future looking like from where you are sitting now based on what you know is important to you. But it makes you wonder, *Have these counselors met live teenagers?*

The answer to any inquiry should always be a positive outlook when communicating with colleges (and honestly in life, too, if you can manage it). Whether it's via an email, on the application questions, or in person, that university your kid is interested in needs to be made aware that his or her future is so bright, you might have to wear a visor! Sorry, 1980s fashion flashbacks have become part of my schema, I think.

Positivism, though, is a standard across the board. Have you ever hung out with a complaining, negative person for a while? They are exhausting. And not at all fun. Most of us prefer to be around shiny, happy people, like REM told us to do back in 1991. Colleges pick up on positivism when it's genuine. We all like to be around positive people with a vision for the future that makes us inspired—except when we just want to lie on the couch, eat chocolate, and watch *The Crown*. Somehow these kids must create a grand vision of their future . . . while playing *Mortal Kombat* and studying for a Spanish test.

I am aware that sometimes too much positivity is annoying. Finding the balance between bubbly and pragmatic is not easy, but it is a must for students. I've read essays from angry students; they do not come across well. I had one student, Becca, who wrote her college essay about how her high school was too hard on her for minor infractions—you know, like cutting class and cheating, the "minor" things. It was a scathing attack on the staff, and the worst part was it was a grammatical mess. If your kid is going to call people out on bad behavior, he or she needs to do it with proper grammar. No college would have looked at that essay favorably. Angry people are not fun, and for pity's sake, proofread!

FIVE
Rank and File

Any parent who has a child in high school (maybe even middle school) has likely had some exposure to the college rankings: a categorized collection of data on colleges and universities detailing which schools are the best in each area of study and where they fall in terms of individual criteria used to rank them. It's like *National Geographic's Field Guide to North American Birds*, only for higher education. I know this because I am old and bird-watching is no longer something I poke fun at but rather something I enjoy and my kids now poke fun at me for doing. For colleges and universities, *US News & World Report* puts out the most well-known book of rankings each year with research done by Robert Morse, the professional most known in this field—or the only person who wants the job.

Morse has been doing research of higher education for more than two decades, and, in an interview, he explained how the rankings are done using criteria " . . . based on 15 indicators, [including] a reputation survey, admissions data, faculty data, financial-resources data, alumni giving, and graduation and retention rates."

This report does not compare all schools; instead the schools are divided into categories, such as liberal arts and national universities, and each variable is weighted. So, reading the rankings is not like having a conversation with your neighbor about a particular school; it's more of a math problem and categorical analysis. Bring some wine and/or chocolate. This collection of information is not fun or easy to review but can be helpful. I think it's important to understand what the rankings are and what they decidedly are not. They are a helpful tool to determine what each university offers based on the opinions of *some* in the industry; they are not a biblical prediction of where your kid should go to college.

But Mr. Morse has been at this a long time, so he must be right about most of these categories, right? I would say that his methodical approach is clean and verifiable but may not tell you much about how your kid will fit in at any given campus. I mean no disrespect to Mr. Morse or to math, but the rankings are the single-most stress-inducing part of preparing for college, and parents and students get sucked into worrying about things they may never have thought about nor need to. There is something about this research that sends parents Googling [is this a word yet?] and researching whether their kid makes the grade for the highly ranked institutions. News flash: Most do *not* qualify for the highest-ranked universities and *that is okay*.

Rank is such a peculiar word, too. We use it to categorize and judge into a hierarchal position, as Morse does; but as a word, it also means "very unpleasant." Something smells *rank* when it has a terrible odor, like a faulty septic system or horse farm. Considering the rankings are compiled with a fair amount of opinion and subjectivity, I think the latter might be more accurate.

Often I sit down for a first meeting with a student and their parent(s) simply to assess how much damage these rankings have caused. Sometimes it's obvious, and the book is on the dining room table like a clunky placemat. At this point, I usually let out an audible sigh, which only the dog seems to understand. Sometimes it's also evident from the way the parent and child interact with one another; rankings can make for some ugly exhibitions. Take Rachel's mom, for example. Rachel wanted to attend Loyola; it was her top choice. But her SAT scores were not as high as others', so her mother, who was getting increasingly nervous with each week that passed, said in an excruciating, high-pitched verbal vomit, "I don't know why you are even applying to some of those schools—you don't have the grades or the scores. You will never get in!" I know parents get upset sometimes, and I try to remain neutral, but my eyebrow had a plan all its own as it jumped up to protest.

Instead of responding, though, I focused on getting a true answer for my student and calming her mom. A small amount of research showed that, yes, Loyola prefers an SAT score over 1310 and Rachel had one of about 1200. She was running out of time to retake the test and was not confident she could do much better. Rachel had missed a lot of school due to her late-stage Lyme disease and its complications, but she was a good student, nevertheless. Loyola was ranked 104 in the college rankings that year, which is relatively high considering there are thousands of colleges, so I understood the mom's concern (though wondered if the next two weeks of eye-rolling and teenage-girl drama was worth stating it aloud). What I found out was that, despite their high ranking, Loyola at the time took students with SAT scores as low as 1100, and Rachel's average grades were in line with their requirements, even a bit higher. She didn't have every piece at the level they wanted, but Rachel's transcript and package were in the range of what Loyola had accepted in the past. Fast forward: Rachel applied and was accepted to Loyola, and her mom has since regained her composure. I'm not completely sure she took my advice, but it's possible wine and/or chocolate were involved.

This sort of scenario is not unusual for me to witness; the rankings can sometimes cause needless stress in a household and result in students (and their parents) thinking they don't have what it takes to get into *any* of the "highly ranked" colleges. To reiterate: There are *thousands* of colleges, many of them wonderful and competitive with more than basic offerings and phenomenal professors, even if you have never heard of them. When we are given a list telling us which ones are "best," it skews our perception, which is problematic in many cases, because suddenly it seems there are precious few "good" colleges and your kid spent the summer sleeping till noon and suntanning instead of shadowing a heart surgeon or building houses for the homeless. Oh, the horror!

One more time—because it's important, but also because I tend to forget what I've said aloud and what I've only thought in my head: There are thousands of good colleges in the United States (and elsewhere for that matter). It's similar to picking a hotel for vacation. I might check out the upscale, modern one with the indoor, heated pool and breakfast buffet, where they put mints on the pillows and give you fresh robes to wear after your shower. I love those robes! In the end, though, the better value might be the Red Roof Inn near the attractions, with the king-size bed and no pool. Most of the time, I never get to the pool anyhow; I end up plopping on the comfy bed and getting sucked into reruns of *The Love Boat* and passing out with a plastic cup branded with the hotel logo in hand. All the extra money for the better hotel often goes wasted in my case.

Money is even more important in the college selection scenario, because the price tag is reminiscent of the days when parents could look at the Louis Vuitton bags or Manolo Blahnik shoes (even if we couldn't afford them), you know, the days before children. Now we all want our children to be happy and have an exceptional college experience, which is like eight thousand pairs of Manolos and fifteen thousand Louis Vuittons. We lose sight of how much tuition costs, because it's for our child, but tuition is likely to continue to be designer-level expensive for the foreseeable future. (You'd think a college education with its price tag would come with a pair of Manolos at least. I don't know who's running this show, but they need to provide more incentives in my opinion.) Though the financials may not be the first thing you look up about a college, ultimately it is an important factor. Some universities give more money in grants and scholarships than others, so a college that starts out thirty thousand dollars more might end up being less in the end.

There is a great article from *The New Yorker* called "The Trouble with College Rankings" by Malcolm Gladwell. I highly recommend reading the whole thing, but I will be quoting it here, because Gladwell seems to say all the things I am thinking about rankings, only with more eloquence and more, well, rank. He begins with, "Rankings depend on what weight we give to what variables." The rankings could change based on the weight given to the categories. And who's to say which categories are most important? You are.

This idea is sort of like ranking restaurants and includes about the same success rate. It's too subjective. Have you ever read a review or had a friend tell you a restaurant has such wonderful "ambiance" only to find that it's basically just poorly lit and you can't see the stupid menu or what the hell you're eating? In addition, when it comes to money, ranking is difficult because it's not just about what the price tag says; it's about what the "value" is, which is also subjective. Is the pasta station really worth the extra cash or does the laundry service make it worthwhile? Maybe it's the updated dorms or the new head of a program your child wants to major in. Many of the items "ranked" are subjective and even ambiguous. Other items are like comparing apples to oranges. How do you compare a school that has thirty thousand students to one that has five thousand? The differences are enormous, and they can't possibly teach the same way or provide the same type of environment.

Value for the money is an included criterion of the rankings, but perspective is key when browsing these "helpful" lists. Notice I said "browsing." College rankings should not be studied or committed to memory or, dear God, read before bed. It's more like a phone book than a Margaret Atwood novel. It's good to use it as a tool, but not get lost in its alluring pages filled with imaginative nightmares. The latest rankings come out each September, the same time everything else happens: school starts, applications are due, college essays are written, SAT/ACT tests are taken, and so on. The rankings are part of the greater whole of college preparatory materials. You know, like this book; only in this book I don't rank anything, except maybe whether white or red wine helps more when kids are being their wonderful, exhausting, contestable selves.

Another important point to consider about the rankings is that about 25 percent are based on a school's reputation. There is no data for this. It's similar to hiring a plumber: You have no idea if the guy who shows up will be clean, respectable, knowledgeable, and skilled, or if he will screw up your pipes and show his butt crack. Malcolm gives an opinion on this as well: "There's no direct way to measure the quality of an institution—how well a college manages to inform, inspire, and challenge its students." I would heartily agree with that and go one further: There's no way for any outside source to determine the best fit for *your* child. Where will your kid engage and feel comfortable yet challenged? Which campus will help your kid feel safe to explore options and try new things?

The rankings create a new set of questions and confusion as you look deeper into them. Does teaching salary translate to better teaching? Some extremely large universities have outstanding faculty, which they tout, yet most students never see them, because TAs (teaching assistants), who make extraordinarily little money but don't traipse off on sabbaticals every three months (mostly because they don't get paid for those), do most of the teaching. Many variables are unknown unless specifically explored, like campus libraries. Do they appear in the rankings you're checking? What about sports? Is a District 1 (D1) school better for a student who wants to major in business? (The National Collegiate Athletic Association labels schools by districts—D1, D2, D3—to indicate which offer the greatest competition and which have the biggest budgets. D1 is the highest level.) Of course only you and your student can answer those questions, and that's the point. What do you and your potential college student care about most? Do the library hours or division statuses matter at all? Or is it more about being in the city, having an acapella club, and small classes? That is personal and individual and does not necessarily connect to the rankings. The mission is to get out of your clam of a kid what's important, what makes him or her feel comfortable—what the Manolo Blahnik is for him or her. Your kid won't know who that is, but perhaps will understand the concept. They have, after all, taken the SATs. (Yep, that was a joke. SATs serve more to confuse and kill confidence than any other one marker I can think of; more on that in the next section.)

Top 10 Things to Know About Rankings:

1. Consider the word rank before looking at college rankings.

2. Bird-watching is now an acceptable pastime for parents, despite wise cracks from young people.

3. Rankings are done with weighted categories; be sure you and your kid even care about those categories before stressing over them.

4. Ranking anything is subjective. Stay away from "subjective" during this process as much as possible; although, I suppose even that comment is a bit subjective . . . sigh.

5. Not all successful people attended a "highly ranked" college or university.

6. Get the facts before telling your kid to give up on school. And him- or herself.

7. There are thousands of good colleges. For real.

8. Consider "value" instead of the "Top 10" according to the Internet; well, except for this list, I guess.

9. Most of us do have to give up on the Manolos, sadly.

10. The college for your kid might not be impressive to everyone. Be impressed anyway.

SIX
Testing, 1, 2 . . . 47 Times

Part of my test-prep coaching has always involved this question: How do you feel about this test? When students think about the tests, most often I find a lot of resistance, obviously. Who can blame them? The SAT was originated in 1926, called the Scholastic Aptitude Test (SAT) and at one point was dubbed the SAT Reasoning Test, which I think is a more accurate moniker. But those early brandings tell me this test was designed to assess *how* you think more than *what* you know. And that is still the case in my opinion.

This is an important distinction, because most students and parents genuinely believe standardized testing says something about a student's intelligence. It might, but the SAT and other standardized tests are not IQ tests, and the resistance to them can prohibit the ability to ascertain a true designation of what a child knows. The SAT assesses how well a student can analyze and solve a problem. This means the questions on these tests are not merely questions to be answered, but rather problems to be solved. That seems like I'm picking at semantics, which I do enjoy, but there is truth in this too.

The way a student thinks about the test could determine how well he or she does on it. At the least it is a determining factor in the outcome. It's like the food we say we don't like, but in all honesty we haven't eaten that food in so many years that we don't know if we like it or not, only that we didn't like it (or wouldn't try it) when we were young. We all have these foods; mine was peas. I hated those little, pasty green balls. Then, in my forties, I think, I decided to try them . . . again, most likely because I wanted to make a dinner that was quick and easy, and my choices were limited because I also hate food shopping and hadn't gone in two weeks. But when I retried peas, I realized I like them (or my taste buds were as old and tired as the rest of me and didn't care anymore). I had spent so many years dissing the peas but hadn't bothered to ever try them beyond the age of five. Imagine if we were all beholden to the choices of our five-year-old selves; we'd be eating Cap'n Crunch and watching *The Flintstones* all day, which sounds better to me than it should, I think. The point (which is getting murkier by the minute, I am realizing) is that it wasn't that I didn't like peas; it was how I thought about the peas that was causing my aversion, not the food itself. It's like that overused and annoying mantra, "What you resist persists." So, basically, taking the SAT or ACT is like retrying peas.

Still, students hate these tests and parents stress over the preparing, performing, and scoring of them. My student, Lily, is a good example. In the middle of our session, she turned her head toward the glass doorway that led to her backyard and considered the birds in the birdbath for several seconds, and then the glaze over her brown eyes glistened in the stream of the sunlight. And . . . she was gone. As a tutor, I know when I've lost a student. Thankfully it doesn't happen too often, but when it does, it's usually during test preparation. I have yet to meet one kid who liked, enjoyed, or appreciated the standardized tests.

Of course, they are kids, so they likely wouldn't appreciate testing regardless of its delivery method, but certainly this test is one of the most difficult parts of preparing for college. I ran an informal survey of my students, and nearly 78 percent of them said the SAT and ACT test ranked in the top three of their "worst parts of preparing for college." It's like an early morning marathon for the brain; they must prepare, but can't prepare fully, and their entire future education depends on how well they do on it. No pressure!

Currently the tests have been made optional by many colleges due to the coronavirus pandemic, but it's worth discussing, because these tests are like the Terminator: They'll be back. They generate too much money as a business for them to disappear. Throughout my years tutoring, I worked with students on improving their test scores. Scores carried a lot of weight in the decision-making process of admissions counselors. I found if my students scored in the 1450 range on the SAT (out of 1600), generally they got into their first-choice school, even if it was a reach school (a reasonable reach school, not necessarily an Ivy, given their standing with the other criteria).

Before you rush off to sign your kid up for a class or hire a tutor, however, I'm also going to share that *very few* of my students got those scores. For the record, it's not because I suck at helping them. A score of 1450 on the 1600-point SAT puts a student in the 97th percentile, which basically means only 3 percent of the test takers in that group scored higher. That small integer is also the percentage of Americans who are living a "healthy lifestyle" according to a Mayo Clinic study. I don't know about you, but that makes me feel much better about my hours of Netflix couch squatting and frequent yearning for Doritos.

To illustrate the point: In 2018, out of 2.13 million test takers, 53,710 scored 1450 or better, which is only 2.5 percent of that group. That's what you're left with after they've taken out all the yummy fatty parts of milk; it's also the number of telemarketers who have success on their cold calls—yet, they persist. It's low. It's a small number of students—and it doesn't matter much. Yes, I said it. In my opinion these tests are carrying less weight every day.

The first, the SAT, was developed by a man named Carl Brigham, who gave IQ tests to millions of army recruits in the World War 1 era. After the war he became a psychologist and taught at Princeton and made a different kind of IQ test that was more difficult and used in 1933 to give scholarships to academically gifted boys (no girls allowed in those days). Why am I telling you all this? So you can consider that perhaps a test made only for very intellectual and academically gifted *boys* in the interest of military service should not be used to judge the readiness for college of the entire young population one hundred years later. It's like if everyone had to take medical exams for health class or presidents had to take a civics test before their inauguration. The latter would certainly be an interesting experiment though.

Test taking is a skill, so students must have the right test-taking habits in addition to having knowledge of the subject matter and an ability to deduce and think critically across a great many subject areas. They need to employ all this proficiency (if they are lucky enough to have acquired it) in a stark, fluorescent-lit, monitored classroom where the energy is like that of an operating room during a life-or-death surgery. They're probably wondering if it's punishment for something. I liken it to standing in line at the grocery store behind the elderly couple who has 834 coupons, moves at the rate of partnering sloths, and pays by check. I suppose on some level we all collectively accept these little miseries of life and now our children must as well. Personally I wish they would get rid of the tests for good. This type of measuring is limited in scope, and many smart, talented kids get left in the academic dust. Alas, no one asked me.

If the tests continue to be required, then students must weigh the options, but there are more options now than there have ever been. They include the following:

Test-optional schools. Hundreds of schools consider test scores if you send them, but students are not required to do so.

Specialized programs. Some of these, such as those for music or art majors or students with a sports focus, won't be concerned about the test scores if those students show they can maintain a minimum GPA.

Community college first. Many community colleges will not need to see SAT or ACT scores for admission; students can often transfer from there based on their performance at community college (this is a great way to find more scholarships, too).

Likely, the 3 percent and several others will need or wish to take the tests because they are pursuing an Ivy League or Top 10 school. But for some students the testing might not be worth it. I discovered that some students are predisposed to a better score based on how their brains work rather than simply a matter of practical knowledge. In truth this was less of a "discovery" and more of an exhausted mom seeing the forest for the trees during a brief, exasperated moment of surrender.

She was me, of course. Ryan was getting ready to take the SAT, and I had never seen his homework, mostly because he did it on the bus ride home, but suddenly I was much more involved in his academics than he was used to. He hated to study but was blessed with a quick mind and great memory. His father and I each enlisted a tutor to help him prepare for the testing: One tutor he didn't like because of his terrible personality, which seemed believable because the dog didn't even like that guy, and the other one was, well, me. Clearly, neither worked out.

I had resigned myself to the idea that his first attempt at this test would be a colossal failure and then, perhaps, I could convince him to get help and better prepare for the next go at it. Instead, my son scored over 2000 (out of the 2400 test at that time), a remarkably high score for his lack of time and effort, putting him in the 95th percentile. I was annoyed-happy, but happy. Jess, on the other hand, gladly accepted tutors and even *my* help to prepare for the tests (she took both SAT and ACT), which she took four times each. She never scored above a 1100 (out of the same 2400 at the time). I share this not to brag or complain, although I'm super at both of those things; I say this as a small reminder: Every single child is different, and these tests are essentially all the same. That contradiction causes a lot of stress in any household when something important is on the line. I'm sure if you are reading this book, you are already aware.

For some students, their brain already works in a way that makes these types of tests easier; I call it Game Show Brain. It's not an official term . . . yet. Standardized testing requires deductive reasoning (among other things) that some game show contestants seem to naturally employ. You hear them working out the answer live on TV sometimes: "Well, if the year was 1600 Europe, then it can't be answer C. Shakespeare was writing *Hamlet*, so it's not A." They rattle off the ridiculous bits of nonessential information they are working through in their brains, none of which you had in your brain, and then they *deduce* the answer. Deduction is one of the essential skills needed for taking the SAT and ACT.

Testing is also an ability to remember in a very particular way, which not everyone can do. There is a need to group or "chunk" information and determine time or setting or the purpose the author has for writing a piece, for instance. Ryan has Game Show Brain. Jess does not, yet she can decipher story lines and follow complex plot and character twists, usually knowing the various possible endings of the story before she reads or sees it. Her brain is fit for immersion and creativity, so it's no shock that she is an artist: She sings, plays instruments, sketches clothing, learns languages, and writes stories, understanding and building exceptional story arcs and character growth. I say this to brag, but then I remember those skills didn't serve her in the world of corporate cubicle jobs and standardized testing. My son's logical brain gave him an edge before he even began to prepare. Or, in his case, didn't. Suffice it to say, he is still great at game shows.

So what happens to the creative or any other kid who does not have Game Show Brain? What if he or she can't make it through the mental gymnastics of trick questions and hours-long intensity? Most do fine. As I mentioned earlier, my daughter majored in a specialized music program for vocal performance at a mid-level college that happened to have a stellar music conservatory on campus. She was able to keep her GPA high enough to keep her scholarships and passed all her classes, earning a Bachelor of Music from Hartford University in Connecticut.

Another student of mine, Terry, could not score above 1000 on the SAT (out of the 1600 test) after three tries. Three is usually when you know this is about the score, unless some serious study and practice is employed. Her score did improve with each try, but the anxiety the test provoked in her was more than she could handle. Her mom wasn't faring well in this situation either. Each time I arrived, her hair contained grayer patches and her speech became more anxious. I didn't know her well enough to recommend day drinking, so instead I showed them the hundreds of schools and universities that are now test optional, such as, University of Chicago, Texas A&M, and Skidmore. Good schools are becoming test optional, more every year, so students (and their beleaguered parents) who can't or don't want to deal with the stress of testing can take heart.

It is okay to opt out if that is what's best for your child. Every case is unique, and every student thrives in different environments. If the testing is too stressful, how would a kid do in a school that wants high test performers? I refuse to believe that a child's entire future rests on the performance of one test. It is not my experience either. Other universities are adopting a "test flexible" option, allowing students to submit different credentials in place of test scores. My student Bella is an extremely creative and bubbly person; you can't help but be happy around this kid. Her test scores, however, were not to love. Bella wanted to go to Emerson but thought she couldn't possibly meet their test score requirements. However, Emerson, along with many other schools now, offers an optional assignment to submit in place of test scores. I love this idea and so did Bella. She made an entertaining and funny video, showing all the wonderful skills she possesses, and it earned her an acceptance to Emerson.

I believe the testing tide may be shifting, so don't fret too much over these or let your child feel bad about him- or herself, because then he or she disappears into a phone and only grumbles and shrugs when spoken to. It's like living with an aging Winston Churchill.

Some schools also allow AP scores or SAT Section tests scores in place of SAT scores for certain programs, or they sometimes waive test scores in favor of a GPA minimum. Again, these insane Olympic-sport-for-the-brain tests are not IQ tests, nor an indicator of a person's dedication or his or her tenacity. How far a student goes is not determined by test scores. They can still fail horribly at life even if they ace the SAT; though that sounds much less comforting than I had intended it.

I had another student, Javier, who had dyslexia. Javier could not take the SAT or ACT due to his limited abilities in reading. But he didn't stop there, and he isn't stopping short of his goals either. He impressed me with his self-taught method of reading by finding key thoughts, writing those down, and connecting the dots later. He would find the words that connected to whatever the story was that he was supposed to read. Many children with dyslexia figure out ways to read in the most amazing and inspiring ways despite their difficulties. Another student with dyslexia I know, Eddie, wrote poetry to help him with reading and writing. These are astounding kids who won't be defined by a test said to be "standardized."

What does *standardized* even mean? I know schools try to create a balanced test that is fair to anyone taking it, but is that possible? Testing is not a reason for you or your child to butt heads. Meet your kid where he or she is, and plan from there. College is competitive, but there are thousands of colleges (have I said that before?). This moment with your child may be hard at times, but try to focus on his or her strengths and on finding the college that best fits for his or her studies as well as for his or her future and life. And now that I know you a bit better, I can also say, consider day drinking.

Sample SAT Questions for Parents

Q: If you're driving a truck at 65 miles per hour through an arc concaved into a mountain, what would the latitude of the crash point be?

A: Questions on the SAT and ACT are designed less like questions and more like problems to be figured out by a process of elimination and deduction. Maybe give your child problems with dinner, like if I toss this dinner roll across the table, what are the chances your sister will catch it?

Q: Shakespeare ate an apple while writing what play?

A: These are not general knowledge tests; students will not know the answers no matter how much they study. They must figure them out with what they do know. Did Shakespeare even like apples?

Q: What are the equivalent coordinates if you want to place yourself in an isosceles triangle-shaped prison to avoid all mention of test prep?

A: The test format, including its structure, length, purpose, validity, or any other aspect, if resisted, becomes harder and chances of success become lower. Sadly, "Suck it up" is a fitting mantra for getting through this experience no matter what type of triangle you're trapped in.

Q: How the *&$k can my kid get a good score on this test?!

A: Preparation and focus are key elements for testing, and practice is essential. Students hate this answer, parents love it. If your kid took music lessons, the process would be similar . . . and just as painful. It begins as, "Did you practice your piano today, Joey?" Three months in, you're shoving a metronome in his face and threatening to take away his video games.

SEVEN

The Dreaded Essay

The basic idea behind the college essay is to communicate growth. Most parents are aware of this goal, so when they try to picture their child writing an essay that doesn't involve video games or TikTok celebrities, they panic. So far, students' knowledge of self is in knowing how many likes their most recent post received or how many marshmallows fit in their mouth at once, so it is difficult to picture them writing an essay that sounds like Socrates.

The last time a teacher asked your child to write about him- or herself, nap and snack time were still daily activities. Remember those "All About Me" projects and dioramas? You know, back when anyone was interested in what your kid *liked* versus what he or she was going to do, be, or produce. Somewhere after elementary school, self-reflective activity seems to mysteriously disappear from the curriculum, giving way to analysis, synthesis, commentary, and persuasion, which are necessary but devoid of philosophical thought; those skills alone do not make well-rounded people. Unless the goal is to rebirth Archie Bunker, some self-reflection can only be beneficial to our society. Sometimes students are even given the position they are to write from. For example, they are asked to write an essay in support of the Mexican–American War, even if they themselves feel the opposite (or they slept through the PowerPoint on the Mexican–American War). While this aspect of the curriculum is helpful for improving analytical skills and critical thinking, it is not much help when it comes time to writing college essays.

Suddenly, as a junior (or senior if your kid is one who procrastinates) students are required to write an essay about themselves in a very truthful, exposing way—the thought of which is terrifying to most of them and their parents. So, if you're thinking, *My kid has absolutely no idea where to even begin* or *My kid is likely to write something embarrassing or stupid,* you're not alone. Truthfully, it's a difficult task for most, if not all, students. They're embarking on a quest for an education trying desperately to be "chosen" by schools that are scrutinizing their credentials when they are too young to have any, and now they must construct an "All About Me" project involving words instead of crazy glue and cotton balls. What could go wrong?

I had a student named Jake who insisted on writing his essay about what he said he'd learned from squeezing cans of tuna over his lifetime. I said, "I'm sorry, say that again?"

"Tuna, you know squeezing out the juice in the cans," he repeated as I winced, because that's what I thought he had said the first time but was hoping I was wrong.

It's not often that I am struck dumb, but there I was: dumb and struck. I thought perhaps I could help him make it funny at least so the admissions counselors would get a laugh and not think the kid was delusional about what constitutes a life skill, but I couldn't find much that was funny about squeezing the juice out of cans of tuna fish. I questioned him about what he had learned from this menial task. "Determination!" he replied emphatically, as if he had already thought about it and was quite proud of himself for coming up with it. Man, I lost sleep over that kid. Eventually, though, I was able to talk him into another topic, thank goodness. He agreed to write his essay on his love of baseball: pure, noncontroversial, and boring. Perfect!

Then there are kids whose stories make me laugh or cry, make me proud, and make me sad to see them go. The reason I do the work I do is because of a college essay written by one of my students, Faraj. (I am assuming by now you have realized I am making up names; this one I chose because it means "remedy or improvement," and I could not think of a more appropriate way to describe his effect on me.) Faraj helped me find my own "calling," so it seemed only right that I learned to do the same for others. Faraj had missed most of his junior year of high school due to surgeries, treatments, and complications with cancer. He was attempting to complete his junior and senior years of school at the same time, while also applying to colleges and working on his dreaded essay. Faraj is an incredibly special person, and because of him, I continue to do this work with a vigor and passion for unearthing truth. We never know the effect of a chance meeting with a stranger.

When this student and I began to work on his college essay, he undoubtedly had a lot to say. I encouraged him to write the whole story, everything he had been through, all the things he was feeling, what he experienced, and how and what he had learned from it all. I had him write the entire story. Eight pages later, he had purged it all onto sheets of handwritten ink covering both sides. I read his personal statement and knew we needed to turn this into his college essay. It was raw and real and gripping, but way too long. So I asked him a simple (well, perhaps not so simple) question: What is the *one* thing you want people to know about you, your story, *this* experience from reading your essay? What should they walk away with?

He thought for quite some time, and then he said, "Cancer is the best thing that ever happened to me."

Boom. There it was: truth. This experience had not belittled him or taken him down. In fact he allowed himself to be educated by it; life instructed him in how to live well. He truly felt the experience of having cancer made him a better person. At seventeen years old, Faraj could take a terrible and terrifying experience and make it a life lesson for himself and everyone he touched, including me. I am so grateful to have been part of that experience.

Once I regained my own composure, I answered him, "Now, *that's* a great first line for your essay." And away we went . . .

The goal is getting students to the college that will feel like home for them, teach them well, and send them off into the world feeling confident and ready and open to opportunities. I realized early on in my business that students need killer essays to accomplish that goal. Not all kids have big medical stories (thankfully!), and essays don't often begin with a slammin' first line like that—hardly ever, in fact. But the personal essay requires a different process from most other essays, and opportunities are bountiful for writing one that gets noticed.

Because the writing is autobiographical in nature, it can be helpful to think in terms of scenes. I ask students to focus on the idea they want to write about and consider what memories come to mind, like the movie version in their heads. What feelings are present (that's always a scary one)—then and now? I ask them to consider if they've made a discovery. Might they have an entirely new thought now that they are older and so much wiser? These are elements that will make up this essay. It's telling the story of their story, even though they don't yet realize they have a story to tell.

I've presented workshops and worked one-on-one with students on the college essay for years, and what I've found to be overwhelmingly true is that writing this essay is (or can be) the catalyst for the entire process of getting to college, and dare I say, doing well while they're there. The idea is simply for them to communicate growth while being genuine and not sound like they've plagiarized an Oprah interview.

As I worked and talked with students privately, I began to understand more about how writing autobiographically presents a challenge for most teens today, because they rarely if ever do it. Usually parents are thinking about the essay before their kid ever shows interest. Most students write only when they are assigned to by their English teacher or when I show up. Once we begin, it goes one of two ways: The essay is already typed and completed, and I'm allowed to look but she doubts she's going to change it much and doesn't really know why I'm there; or the student has absolutely no idea what to write about at all—he has no memories, no problems, no growth, nope, can't come up with a thing. Both are fun and eventually I see in their eyes that spark—it could be the blue light from their laptop, but at least occasionally it means they have an idea.

Cassidy was a brilliant student with a solid essay—she was in the first of the aforementioned groups: Her essay was finished. I liked her essay very much, but she and I both knew it was missing something. She had written about her chronic illness, a strong enough topic, and her writing was solid. Somehow, though, Cassidy wasn't *in* the essay. Of course it was about her, and she is mentioned, but I didn't feel her bubbly and organized personality in her words. One of the important goals of an essay is to have a genuine voice. I had worked with Cassidy for a couple of years prior, so I knew her well. I started questioning why she didn't write about literature or cosplay, some areas I knew she loved and was involved with. But, of course, I understood her need to talk about how she lives and what she's learned from her illness. I wanted to merge the two, and it hit me that she could keep the topic and change the structure. So I said, "How about writing this story as a one-act play?" Spark! There it was. And when she'd finished, hers turned out to be one of my favorite essays.

Another time, I helped a math whiz writing about depression use the number of days she was hospitalized to add numbers to her very personal story. It's exciting for me when this happens, not just because it results in a great essay, but also because students learn something about how to better express themselves. That's a quality they need before they go wherever they go. If they go. Gosh, I hope yours go.

Part of the difficulty of the essay part of the process is how much parents are on the outside looking in. Most students won't even show their essays to their parent(s) until it's complete. Some never do. Kids do understand the gravity of this assignment. In the end, most are better for it—better writers, better thinkers, better humans in some small but not insignificant way.

In my opinion the best way to help kids write their essays is to not help them unless they ask. A discussion can do wonders, but they must start it; otherwise, it's your idea, so inevitably they hate it.

Some Essay Conversation Starters

A. Ask which of their trophies they feel most proud of as a possible topic, but be sure they played that season.

B. Talk about family vacations, but stop the conversation before they decide to write about the six-car pileup they witnessed on I-95 when they were nine.

C. Steer them to genuineness without giving away all the family secrets; no one needs to hear about Uncle John's time incarcerated.

D. Tell them, in this essay, they can finally focus on themselves; this should be a teen's dream come true!

E. Allow them to focus on something smaller if they want—just not squeezing tuna!

EIGHT

Empty Mess

When Ryan, who is my youngest, left for Hofstra University in 2014, I remember feeling lost. He was only one state away, less than three hours without traffic, but we live in the tri-state area, where traffic is synonymous with driving. He was off to study music management, which likely wasn't even a field of study until that decade. My ambivalence aside, I had devoted most of my time (and a more-than-imaginable amount of my energy) to raising children. The "job" I had had for nearly twenty years had suddenly come to an end. My children were now furthering their education.

I had planned for this day since they entered kindergarten—their graduations and ambitions, awards and accolades—but I hadn't given much consideration to what their continuing education meant in terms of *my* life. I wandered around the kitchen looking for messes to clean. I sat on my couch staring at a blank TV screen. I rewashed laundry. All I could think on that first day home alone was, "Damn, it's quiet here!" Because my kids are both musicians, I had grown accustomed to hearing drums, guitar, horns, and operatic octaves at all hours in all rooms throughout the house. Coming through the bathroom, guitar riffs and soprano notes felt like the standing-room-only section at the far end of an opera house. The fact that Jess was singing Mozart's "Queen of Night" aria and Ryan was playing a heavy metal anthem entitled "Snuff" only made the music more entertaining and interesting as the competing sounds greeted each other in the hallway. I always told my kids they should work together on a music project, but then I remembered they couldn't even split the last chocolate chip cookie without an epic battle.

Sitting in silence I began to wonder what the deal was with "empty nest." Is this a syndrome or more of a condition? Should I seek medical help or a good therapist? What I eventually discovered from personal and witnessed experience is . . . it sucks. But only initially. It's like buying this cool new bag and carrying it around everywhere, filling it up with expensive makeup, a leather wallet, an iPhone 12 (or whatever three-digit number they're likely on at this point)—the best of everything; you love this bag and keep it close to you all the time. Then one day someone steals your bag right out from under your nose, and no matter how many years you'd had it, you are bereft and didn't see it coming. So, like me, you are left on a couch in the dark searching for rom-coms to cry over.

Considering how much rom-coms suck, the absence of noise began to feel like an unrequested but generous gift. So when your children return, and you're asked to give back this precious silence, frankly, you're kind of pissed off about it. I know it can be hard to imagine, but for me, I began to relish my evenings on the couch with the sweetest two men I know: Ben and Jerry. The best part was I knew *I* wouldn't leave the spoon stuck to the coffee table. Mine was one type of response to empty nest, there are many other reactions.

There are those wise souls who dance all the way home from the college campus able to contemplate the good times to come. Others eat pints of ice cream for the first several weeks until they come to their senses. Obviously, I was the latter.

I also had time to research during my dark nights, so I let my investigative journalist personality attempt to allay my fears. What I found, according to 2014 census data, was there are roughly 22.5 million empty nest homes in the United States; many parents do suffer some form of loss, but, as I have said (probably ad nauseum at this point) throughout this book: The key to any transition is preparation. I think I read that on a Tony Robbins website, so I figure it must be true. Does anyone have more energy than that man? I want him to have an event where we get to talk about how tired we all are and take naps instead of walk on hot rocks.

Personally, though, I truly found that preparing made the process smoother. When Ryan was leaving, I planned the wonderful things we would do before DO Day (drop-off day; I made this up, because everything seems to have a day and an acronym for it). I thought Ryan and I would shop together for dorm accessories, peruse the campus together, move him in, hang out until the wee hours of the night, and then I'd watch him fall asleep. Clearly, my Disney plans didn't work out. Instead I was home in bed by ten that night, a gift I'm sure Ryan was thankful for. In direct contrast to my expectations of how things "should" go, there was the actuality of busy schedules, out-of-stock dorm supplies, Ryan's greater interest in hanging out with new friends, and the absence of accurate measurements for a refrigerator—"Damn, I really thought it would fit there."

The reality of empty nest is that it is different for everyone. The Mayo Clinic is one source on what to do if you have questions or need help. Mayo addresses the needs of empty nesters, like acceptance, support, and positivity. Acceptance that your child or children are leaving/has left is step one. You can't keep them home; honestly, I don't think you want to. They're messy, smelly, and not that reliable. However difficult, acceptance of this transition is essential. Mayo and others recommend focusing on how you can help your child succeed outside of your home. I think that's a viable suggestion, because if they can't handle it, they will come back—with their disappointment *and* their laundry. Maybe go over with them how to write a proper email, or fill out a check, or locate the spot for the stamp on an envelope. Sadly, each of these examples is real.

Also, seeking support is a key element to overcoming empty nest syndrome. Likely you have some friends who have gone through or are going through a similar experience. My neighbor Connie and I commiserated often. We basically raised our children together and had long talks at the bus stop. We shared our kids' puberty stories, melt downs, and missteps, as well as their accomplishments and celebrations, attending every birthday and religious event for each other.

We chauffeured each other's kids to activities and provided last-minute babysitting. We grew apart in the middle school years with the crowbar of life pulling us in different directions; those are busy years. Once our children went to college, we rekindled our joint need for complaining—uh, I mean, airing our sadness and frustration. We discussed the feelings of emptiness, strangely coupled with an elated feeling of freedom at not having to worry about what's for dinner that one gluten-free, one vegan, and two excessively picky eaters will not huff and eye-roll about. This process may sound negative, but it's more cathartic. I found that when we focused on our children's more annoying traits, it helped us miss them less. It's like what women do after a break-up with a crummy boyfriend: Recall that time he showed up forty-five minutes late without calling, or the umbrella he gave as a birthday present, or calling you some other chick's name. We do this so we can bid him good riddance! After several pints of Häagen-Dazs and hours of Adele.

The idea is that support from friends, family, coworkers, or random people at the grocery store really helps. You'd be surprised at how much people will nod and commiserate with your parenting plights once you tell them. Several grocery store cashiers and I have had many a good cry together over the broccoli. And the support you derive from others helps with that other pesky element needed for coping: positivity.

Although I understand the need for positivity, and have spoken about it often, I've long been annoyed by the constant barrage of books, movies, podcasts, motivational speakers, and TED talks on the power of positive thinking or some similar revelation. It's great to be thinking positively, but is it necessary to be positive when you're not? I have a difficult time being positive about things I am simply not "positive" about. Unless they mean "positive" in the definite sense, like I'm positive I am going to cry every time I watch *A Dog's Purpose*; that is true. But positive as in, everything-is-wonderful-all-the-time positive, not so much.

However, over the years I have discovered that focusing on what is working in my life versus what is not *is* an effective tool. Not better than ice cream, but effective. And there are positive aspects to empty nest. Your feelings will range from loss and maybe sadness to moments of relief and even, dare I say, freedom, as in "I get to hold the remote now" or "I can find the remote now!" So when my children left, I focused on doing things I hadn't had an opportunity to do in a long time, like be naked outside of my locked bathroom. No further visual imagery is needed here.

Psychology Today explains it this way: "Empty nest syndrome refers to feelings of depression, sadness, and/or grief experienced by parents and caregivers after children come of age and leave their childhood homes," which is accurate in my experience, although they left out the part about when said children return to their childhood homes and you've already turned their rooms into a gym/meditation area/

yoga space/office. Whoops. *PT* further describes empty nest as a doctor might, to allay fears: "Empty nest syndrome is not a clinical diagnosis, but rather describes a transition period in which many people experience feelings of loneliness or loss. While many parents encourage children to become independent adults, the experience of sending children off into the world can be a painful one." This explanation offers some clarification. Either way, empty nest is a time of transition, like Tony Robbins and I have said. It's not always a fun time, but I imagine it's better than walking on hot rocks.

Truthfully, I think empty nest syndrome begins before they leave. Even if your kids don't "go away" to school, life is forever changed when they graduate high school. Some parents want to hold on to the feeling of having children who need them versus trying to adjust to having adults in their lives who live somewhere else and somehow still zap their wallet.

I lived alone with my mother next door when my children were both in college, and, though I would have loved to have gone out on the town, I had transferred most of my money to their accounts during the semester and was too broke to go anywhere. Plus, even as a grown-up, I didn't want to explain to my mother where I was going and be subjected to interrogation when I returned home. Funny how the cycle continues!

It's a great idea to plan a nice dinner or an outing with your kids before they go, but try not to pick something you did when they were five and relive a memory of meeting Mickey Mouse or going to a water park. Please . . . don't do that. Perhaps you can find a movie you both would like to see or a concert you both might enjoy. It's an opportunity to build a memory with this person as they are now, not the five-year-old you're mourning, who came to you with scraped knees and goodnight kisses. This person doesn't use Neosporin despite the numerous warnings of risk of infection, and they rarely give you a goodnight kiss anymore—unless you're going to bed, and they're going out for the night and need money or your car.

Once the children leave, if you really are in that melancholy place, haven't showered in three days, and are wearing your mopey sweats, then it's okay to have a night of indulgence and self-pity. Sometimes I would break out the M&M's and ice cream and just have at it. I start with the photo albums; you know you have them somewhere too. When my kids were babies, we took actual photos and displayed them: Jess hanging upside-down from a jungle gym bar and Ryan in a full mummy costume and makeup. Then they grew, and I was too busy for quality photos and colorful frames; technology took over, and my computer became loaded with images of awards, concerts, games, parties, and anything else I could capture. If you were organized enough to take videos, break them out. Now's the time. I revisited each wonderful, terrible stage. The saggy diapers, the potty pitfalls, the first steps . . . all the way to the proms and graduations; I drowned in that crap for a night—the movies and pictures, not the ice cream. Although, that's generally the best part, trying different flavors and adding bananas and whipped cream—whatever you want for your pity party.

Of course it will only remind you of the countless "kiddie" parties you had over the years, which were exhausting and horrible. But at this juncture you will remember them differently: angelic children floating around the park with clean faces and loving each other like cherubs. In reality, most of those kids were running around like maniacs and screaming. Then you might, in the quiet of your home, have the same realization I had: No one else will eat your stashed sweets now, especially if you hide them from your significant other. Yeah, baby. No one will leave an empty container in the freezer, unless it's you—or your spouse if you don't hide your stuff well enough. You see where I'm going with this? There is a silver lining. Cruise down Memory Lane at the speed you drive when a cop is watching, but then get beyond it, like when the cop following you suddenly turns left, and you go straight and speed up. Until, of course, you see that cop again on the cross street two roads up and you're doing seventy-two in a forty.

You have survived all the crazy stages of life with your children; relive them, embrace them, and then let them be. The memories will always be there for you, but the time has come for you to think about your future, too. There are so many new ice cream flavors out there to try.

For me, I started by taking better care of myself. I thought about people and activities in my life that had sort of been on autopilot for the last eighteen years or so. I started with calling some friends. We all had friends before those small people infiltrated our lives and took over like tiny, fascist leaders. I think we even went out sometimes. With friends. Like grown-ups. It's likely a distant memory, but think back, you might find it. Those people are probably as haggard and broke as you are now, but they are also likely still there.

You're going to have an opportunity to reconnect with good friends again, too. Your first thought when you see them will probably be, *Oh my gosh, they're so old.* And the second thought will be, *Oh crap, so am I.* Once you get over that sad realization, it will be awesome to reconnect, mostly. Like when Ryan told me I should watch the series *Stranger Things* because I'd love it and that Winona Rider played the mom . . .the mom! How did Winona get to be old enough to play the *mom?* You see, this is where the ice cream and pizza and *friends* come in. The point is you will have time and the brain space to once again be friends with people and share experiences. Although your brain space is likely damaged from years of child rearing, the great part is so is theirs. You can go out with your damaged brains and enjoy time with friends again. Provided it ends by nine, when you will be in your pajamas.

Other relationships, like partners, benefit from your children leaving the home also. Do you even remember what it was like to be with your spouse or significant other alone? Did you have a wedding with this person? Most spousal interaction when you have children consists of reminding each other to take out the garbage or ask who's picking up which kid from soccer today. The empty nest allows for more room and time with that person you love, or hopefully at least remember. You can have date nights at home, which honestly is where I want to be anyway. You can also have sex anywhere again. However, let me preface that with a warning that age does limit sexual prowess for most of us. For instance, don't try the stairs anymore. It's simply an ER visit you'll have to explain. Most other options still work, and the noise level is no longer a factor. Although do be aware that if your child has a way to return home unexpectedly, it will happen. And it will most certainly be when you decide to be naked, trying some new position. Then you'll pull your back out jumping up and must return to the ER.

If you're not with a partner, then this time might be frightening, because it seems so lonely. In my personal experience, that is somewhat true. While my musical kids were away at school, I kept playing "The Day the Music Died" by Don McLean like a serial killer. "A long, long time ago I can still remember how that music used to make me smile . . ." It was not pretty. But a funny thing happened after a while, and I began to enjoy the quiet that I could fill with other music, or QVC, or the silent reading of a book. As a matter of fact, I could do whatever I wanted, whenever I wanted. Mostly, I did nothing, but still the option was there.

What I did find in my solitude was my creativity. Once you have what's left of your brain back, you can return to creative pursuits you once loved. Maybe you used to play the piano and now can barely finger a C chord. Now you can sit down and realize how out of tune that thing is and how much more it costs to tune it these days. Piano tuning is a dying art, and they charge accordingly. I considered a personal loan to pay for the use of my piano in tune, but realized I had already maximized my debt with two kids in college. So I found a guy who would let me pay in installments. People sometimes take pity on the new empty nester, or maybe it was my sobbing at the bill that changed his mind.

You could also focus on home projects, if that's your thing. Then post them on social media and make everyone else feel bad. That's fun. Essentially you can be creative again; the empty nest is a free pass to do things you've always wanted to do. Okay, maybe not climb Mt. Everest, because, unless it's gotten a lot smaller in the last twenty years, it's probably going to be too much. For instance, I took a hike on Bear Mountain in Arizona recently with my son. He decided to take the most challenging path, which seemed like a good idea at the time, but turned out to be hours of iced legs and uninterrupted napping later. I finally found my way out, after eleven and a half hours, with a broken shoelace and an empty water bottle. Someone needs to mark those trails better, and there should be escape options every mile.

Mountains notwithstanding, you can do many things that do not require quite as much conditioning. Join a gym or take up yoga. I returned to a yoga practice, however my body did not join me. The experience was a lot of falling over and sitting in child's pose. Maybe you want to paint or bake or organize your closets. If the latter is something you're into, please get in touch with me. My closets are primed for an episode of *Hoarders*. Maybe you're thinking about creating an office space with a *Star Wars* theme or designing furniture shaped like animals; whatever it is, you can take it seriously now.

You won't be running to and from games, practices, college visits, and kids' events, so when you find yourself driving around aimlessly crying and listening to "Cat's in the Cradle," pull over at a yard sale and find some junk to repurpose. Whatever you choose to do, be sure you create a beginning to go with this ending. I don't want to sound like a greeting card, but though this change is hard, each ending opens the door to something new. So, before the new thing becomes joining your mom's mah-jongg club, dear lord, pick something *you* like to do.

When you can't figure out what to do, there is another option: Do nothing. Can you imagine taking a break? Think back, it's there somewhere. You can do that. Instead of filling every minute of every day, take a minute or two to relish sitting in a chair or walking to the mailbox—slowly. Sometimes it turns into dancing or cooking or baking or planting or some other activity; sometimes it doesn't. I found the inertia uncomfortable at first. I kept thinking I ought to be doing something or checking on my kids, but I learned that if I can hold back and let my kids handle their own problems, challenges, and situations without intervention, I might have a life, and they might learn to be functional adults.

One word of advice: If your kids are like mine and handle most of the technology issues in the home, then be sure to get your computer needs addressed before they leave. No joke, I had to find out what the crazy Wi-Fi password was and write it down somewhere. Yes, I'm aware I'm not supposed to write down passwords, but how do people remember them if they don't? Then I wrote it down somewhere else, because I knew I would forget where I had put it. I also wrote down the instructions for how to use it, as told by my children, slowly and in step-by-step sequence, like a wikiHow page. Several times. Once you have all the information you can squeeze out of your kids, find an IT person who doesn't break the bank before they go.

You need working computer systems, but you also need money for the spa, where you can go now. Alone. The first time I went to the spa without my daughter, I thought they had forgotten to charge me for stuff. I was almost afraid to ask why the bill was so low. Oh, I see, her mani/pedi, haircut, low lights, wax, and massage really were the reason I was broke all the time. Good to know.

Once your computers are maintained and your photos have been sufficiently sobbed over, dance, sing, boogie, or lip sync in your living room like no one is watching. Because they're not. Unless you count the dog, who already knows your mental state better than anyone and, due to a kind gift from nature, he's not telling. You might cry in the shower. Have a good cry and play your out-of-tune piano, listen to Led Zeppelin up loud, and do crafts at your dining room table. Do whatever you need to do to keep from stalking your college student. I'm not going to say I know this firsthand, but most colleges frown on parents hiding in the bushes.

This was the time when I began to appreciate social media. I could not have cared less about Facebook or Instagram before my kids left for college. Then I realized if my daughter had a green dot next to her name, then that meant she was on Facebook too! Which also meant I could reach out and message her. To her, it meant constant annoying dings on her laptop from Mom, who had another question or reminder: How are you doing? What have you been eating? Are you drinking alcohol??? I soon learned that it was just as effective if I didn't communicate with her though. I could go on social media anytime and see when she was last on. If she posted thirteen minutes ago, I knew she was alive! Genius! I could suspend all the horrific thoughts that occurred when my text to her didn't receive an answer in the three seconds since I sent it. Those are a long three seconds: *Oh my God, she must be in a ditch somewhere, or at the bottom of the lake, or somehow became involved with a drug cartel* . . . the list of terrors is endless.

When I felt that panic coming, I would go over to my computer and ask Facebook what she was up to. And there it was, like a Magic 8 Ball on my computer screen. *Facebook, is Jess okay?* Well, let's see, she was online just seven minutes ago, so yes, it appears she is alive and well. *Awesome!* This, of course, will change constantly, but online tracking seems to be here to stay, so parents can take heart that they will be able to stalk their children quietly from the privacy of their own home.

I think what parents really want is to maintain some control. Oh sure, we worry, and of course it's because we'd like to keep our children safe. But it's also because we had gotten used to focusing so much on their lives that we didn't focus on our own. In the words of Erma Bombeck, "When mothers talk about the depression of the empty nest, they're not mourning the passing of all those wet towels on the floor, or the music that numbs your teeth, or even the bottle of capless shampoo dribbling down the shower drain. They're upset because they've gone from supervisor of a child's life to spectator. It's like being the Vice President of the United States."

Amen, Erma, amen.

Music List for Empty Nesters

"The Day the Music Died" by Don McLean, in case, like me, you want to go there.

"Forever Young" by Rod Stewart, or the other one by Bob Dylan, who wrote everything before anyone else).

"A Mother's Prayer" by Celine Dion, who makes me cry even when I don't know what she's saying.

"Child of Mine" by Carole King; yikes, am I that old!?

"Simple Man" by Lynyrd Skynyrd, because I refuse to be old *and* not cool.

"To Zion" by Lauren Hill, this one makes me think of my son, because Zion and Ryan kind of rhyme—or when you're depressed you change the words to suit you.

"I Hope You Dance" by Lee Ann Womack, because I'm cool enough for Skynyrd but I'm also corny.

All these will likely make you cry, but Lauren Hill will make you dance while you're crying.

Wine and chocolate are recommended.

NINE

Hey, Buddy, Can You Spare Some College Tuition?

Dave Barry once said, "I believe we parents must encourage our children to become educated, so they can get into a good college that we cannot afford." If you have begun the college search and perused the tuition tabs on university websites, it's very likely you agree with Dave.

Parents want to provide an education for their kids. It's a noble cause, but mostly they do it because they want to know that eventually their kids will get out and pay their own electric bill. Maybe then they will finally shut off the damn lights.

Consider whether living at home is an option for your child, maybe at a state or community college, which would certainly lower the price but may also raise your blood pressure. It's a constant weighing of options to find the least terrible.

When my kids were young, I saved for their education, yet in eighteen years I barely had enough for a 1992 Datsun in fair condition no less four years of college at today's prices. It's no secret: College is expensive. Now, after financially helping two kids get their degrees and countless others to make choices, I realize the total cost of college was more than I'd spent on our family home or anything in my lifetime. I didn't want to whine about it too much, but my kids are both creative artists and studied music in college, so I couldn't tell myself, *Once they begin their fulfilling full-time work as a heart surgeon it will all be worthwhile!* It might be more like, *Once they join the gig economy and don't have health care options, get paid low wages for performance and creative endeavors, and find that supplementary part-time job they hate, maybe they might be able to pay their loan payments, if nothing goes wrong.* I can't say that was comforting, but what I would say is they studied what they love and grew into very fine conscientious, self-aware young adults . . . who are still poor. They also still live at home, but that's another story entirely.

Regardless of what your kid decides to study, it's likely college will cost a lot of money. It will also come with little guarantees. It's an investment not unlike the stock market in my opinion, dependent upon a range of economic factors and public health. Since the pandemic, we've learned that those variables can tear down an economy, but that we can also restore jobs and raise wages in that same amount of time. It's a like a roller coaster without the fun. None of us knows what's ahead, so we keep plugging along with hope—and drink wine.

With all that in mind, it might be time to change our perspective about what purpose college serves for our children. Realizing a BA or a BS is not necessarily a ticket to a well-paying and stable position changes the game. In my experience I've seen hundreds of students, and overall young people seem to want fulfillment *and* money. Greedy buggers, aren't they?

These days it's a tough combination when realistic choices for them begin with Walmart greeter or unpaid intern. More and more young people (and many adults for that matter) are working a few part-time jobs to gain expertise or make rent while they figure it out. Some are lucky and have chosen a field in which they get a job at graduation. Either way, they find something and begin their journey after college, whether they know what it looks like or not. It's like watching unathletic kids from the bleachers and praying they get the ball and don't completely mangle the play. And then taking them out for ice cream either to celebrate or to heal the wounds. But they can't eat ice cream forever. Truthfully, I'm still using it as a coping mechanism, so maybe they can, but it won't help their financial situation.

As parents, it's important to remember that this is a "journey" and not a quick, painful event that we can close our eyes and click our heels to exit. *The Wizard of Oz* has given us false hope about challenging events, as well as the possibility of getting to the man behind the curtain and having him change his ways. Difficulties will arise no matter what major or degree kids choose. My son waited until sophomore year of college to announce that he didn't need a degree that cost nearly six figures to become a music producer or manager and declared he was "done with college" and planned to quit. That was certainly a wine and chocolate kind of day, but once I regained consciousness, I realized flying off the handle would be fruitless. Plus, I had a hangover at that point, and even thinking about yelling made my eyes tear. So I placated him with Pop-Tarts (his childhood favorite) and climbed aboard my rickety soap box to give him more of the advice he did not want.

At this age he only allowed me short bursts of attention, so I spoke in earnest and without judgment—well, as much as a mother can be nonbiased when her kid is making a terrible decision, which is to say not . . . at . . . all. I had to somehow defend the expenditure, though I, too, thought it was a hefty price tag for an indefinite return.

He was right on that count, because when he and his sister were both in college, I sort of lost track of the total cost. It was as though every time we turned around some other charge had been added to the bill. It seemed like there was a fee for everything: library fee, technology fee, bathroom fee, walk-the-pavement fee, even a look-we-planted-hydrangeas fee. I think my brain just shut off somewhere around ninety thousand dollars. I thought if I acknowledged an extra digit, it would have sent me into full anaphylaxis. I find when something is too much or too big to wrap my brain around, I split it up in my head. So, in my mind, the bill becomes 4 "easy" payments of twenty-three thousand dollars, like an infomercial for Ginsu knives you see at three in the morning. Self-help gurus say it all the time: Break large, unmanageable goals into smaller, more achievable chunks. Even Weight Watchers agrees with this tactic so that their patrons don't get on the scale hoping to have miraculously shed eighty pounds in ten days when they've been living on Easy Mac and eclairs.

I used this same tactic with money for college; however, I did continue to buy mac 'n' cheese, admittedly. It's difficult for parents and students to imagine how the finances will work out. I reminded Ryan (and myself) that college was, in fact, a choice. It didn't always feel that way, and I admit to starting early in their school years planning and talking about college as if it were a given for them. In my defense, I lived in a time when a kid could work a part-time job, live at home, and afford to pay for college themselves. Now they live away to have the experience of moving out without any cost to them directly. Why didn't our generation think of this? It's totally genius!

Yet, there is still the matter of paying for it. What I realized, however, was that this dilemma was also an opportunity to teach my kids about money. We make choices every day about money: *How much do I want to make? Should I buy those shoes? Is thirty-two dollars in shipping too much?* These are valuable lessons, and kids don't learn them anywhere else. I am not a financial advisor, so I won't give advice, but I will say, college is a wonderful opportunity for teaching fiscal responsibility to your kid. Or, in my case, for aimlessly trying to explain to your child why he cannot go to Miami University (even though he got in) because he didn't get any scholarships. Frustrating as it may be, prepping for college is a good time to get serious with your kid about money. Together you can do the homework on loans, grants, and scholarships so colleges won't sell you the Ferrari package when you're on the Smart Car budget. The point is that they should know. Kids shouldn't be shielded from the financial part. Even though their part-time gig delivering pizza likely won't get them through even a semester on campus at their top-choice school, savings toward that education will help them in the long run. You know, when you begin charging them rent and they are indignant about paying for the room where they have always hoarded glasses and spoons for free.

I say this not because I am so knowledgeable or that my children went through this process seamlessly, but because my daughter didn't take any of my sound advice and embarked on a master's degree right after undergrad. I spoke, she ignored, and now she has exceptionally high student loans and no master's degree. Things happen, and sometimes life twists and turns while all we can do is hang on for dear life. I think kids want to be independent, but it's hard when everywhere around them is a scam or a trick waiting to catch them. Also, it's hard to pry themselves away from the video games and dinner magically appearing on the table when they hit pause. Jess is still pursuing her dreams and working as an artist. It's a choice she doesn't regret, but she acknowledges the financial aspect will plague her for a long time to come. I watch and worry, but I don't judge, and I don't say, "I told you so." Too much.

If kids don't learn the financial zigzags life can take, they are setting themselves up for disappointment, and it will be a rude awakening when their loan officer calls four years later. We know children don't listen to warnings of what might occur down the road. They have no capacity to see past the TikTok video trending or the paper they have due on Saturday. They think, *I'm eighteen! I can build credit by borrowing!* Oy!

It's like looking into a tunnel with your kids and seeing a bright light. They think, *Oh, how pretty, I must go into the light.* Meanwhile, you are shaking your head and screaming, "Get out of there! It's a train coming!"

Still, most parents want to provide an education for their kids; we are hardwired for it, though I'm unclear who did the wiring. It's a noble cause to want your children to be educated. It's also the only way you see them ever paying their own cell phone bill. I know near-thirty-year-olds still on their parents' plan. Oh wait, that's my kid. In any case, students have choices, likely more than they want or can handle. But there are enough to find not only the "fit" they are looking for in a college but also the financial fit your family needs.

There are thousands of colleges, none of which are "cheap," but some price tags are comparable to a Mercedes and others a prime nineteenth-century chateau in the mountains outside Versailles. Consider your options and then decide which are most realistic for your family. Maybe living at home is an option for your kid. There are great colleges across the country, and it's likely he or she could go to school locally and save on room and board. I know, we want them to experience living away from home, but perhaps there's a basement they could inhabit that would lower the price of college—though it is likely to increase your blood pressure. You constantly have to weigh the options. Maybe they can do a semester abroad or work on campus; see, even more options.

To get back to my son and his split decision to leave college in the second year, I learned in that moment that I had no idea how his journey would play out. Ultimately it was his choice. All I could do was be honest and then bite my tongue. And I was—honest about my fears, honest about money, and honest about employment prospects and fulfillment. My tongue, on the other hand, has a permanent dent. I knew he would have to consider his options and investigate his future for his own answer. I did not have it. He listened, which was a sign of maturity I had not seen in his high school years. Then he took some time, talked with some trusted friends in the same boat, and decided to continue with school. He also forgot to tell me of his decision for several days while I bit my nails down to bloody nubs.

Life is bunch of choices with no clear road map. In this big roulette wheel, we choose in a moment and live out the consequences in years. In the case of college tuition, there is no right or wrong answer. It's an investment, and each student must decide how much he or she can or is willing to invest. It's another in the long list of life lessons that come with prepping for college. The stressful path provides moments of bonding and teaching, as well as learning, for both parent and child.

Money tips for your kids before they go to college or wherever they go:

- Starbucks decaf-mocha-latte-with-a-shot-of-espresso-to-stay-awake-and-loaded-with-extra-whipped-cream orders add up quickly; drink tea—hot water is free

- They do not *need* the new shoes/jacket/backpack/whatever; they wear pajamas to class, and they may not even be clean

- Textbooks can be used, purchased online, or borrowed. Tell them to seek cheaper options; they were born after Google

- If their meal card is not enough, they might consider a part-time job to feed themselves (this one usually makes them suddenly less hungry).

- Peanut butter and jelly sandwiches are likely cheaper than fast food; just be *sure* your roommate is not allergic (I speak from experience on this one)

TEN

To ED or Not to ED

Each year several students and parents ask me about applying to college Early Decision, often called "**ED**" for short. And then they promptly ignore my advice and do it anyway. Obviously I am not a big fan of ED, but in certain instances for certain students it can be a good option. Sometimes.

For anyone unfamiliar with the term, ED is one of the options for students to consider when applying to college. The main options for applying are: Early Decision, Early Action (**EA**), and Regular Decision (**RD**). Beginning with the latter, Regular Decision means students must apply by the college's deadline date. They should not do this on the last day, when the system will likely crash because 80 percent of students will also be sending their application on that same day. The advantage of RD is that it gives you the most time to prepare the application; the disadvantage is entering the application pool when it is at its most crowded. With that many anxious young people entering the pool at the same time, it's certain some of them are going to pee in it.

Early Action, or EA, is the middle-of-the-road option, and my personal favorite. Required of EA applications is an earlier due date, but what it offers is a chance to stand out from the crowd by arriving, and likely deciding, early. It's like those diners that charge less for people who are willing to eat dinner at four in the afternoon. Sadly, I'm finding that offer looks better to me every day. Then I can be in bed by nine. Middle age has reverted me to a toddler's eating and sleeping schedule; I'm even prone to tantrums again. It no longer seems like an overreaction to howl for several minutes when someone takes the last cookie and leaves the empty package on the table. The thwarted anticipation of a cookie is not something to be toyed with.

EA means students get a "head start," not points necessarily, but perhaps a closer look. With less in the virtual "pile," admissions employees are likely to spend more time with each packet and/or take a closer look than they will when the pile is filled with the last-minute "laggers." The important element here is that EA does not come with any restrictions, other than to get it in by the earlier deadline. Students don't have to guarantee they will attend the school that accepts them early.

Not so for ED. Early Decision applicants have the stipulation that, should said school accept them, they guarantee they will attend. I've often wondered about the consequences of not complying, but surprisingly, it happens infrequently. Most students who get into their ED schools, go to them. However, if they do change their mind and back out, they risk losing the other offers and acceptances they received from other schools. It becomes an ethical issue and would be a terrible way to start at a new school: Oh, you're the student who wanted the other school and promised them you'd go but then changed your mind and didn't. Eyes roll in unison. It's high school all over again, and we just got out of that nightmare.

For your upcoming nightmare, here's a simple breakdown:

<u>ED Binding</u>
Big commitment
Improve chances of acceptance the most
Can apply to any other schools simultaneously
Must decide and pay early, sometimes before receiving financial aid package

<u>EA Nonbinding</u>
No commitments or restrictions
Improves chances of acceptance
Can apply to any other schools simultaneously
Still have until May 1 to decide

<u>Regular Decision</u>
No commitments or restrictions
No improved chances of admission
Can apply anywhere/anytime simultaneously by the deadline
Have until May 1 for deposit and decision

Let us not forget the newest of the bunch, because, apparently, it wasn't already confusing enough: Single-Choice Early Action (**SCEA**). This is a newer idea to provide some selectivity without the binding contract. For SCEA, students apply to only one college through an Early Decision application. They can apply to others only through Regular Decision application. Less binding, more confusing. It's like those new and improved product commercials: "Try the new Spanx—less binding, more restricting! More than 89 percent of women surveyed say, 'The less binding Spanx is the one for me!'" What???

With EA applications, students are gaining a benefit without giving up much in my opinion. Even SCEA has only the restriction that you can't EA anywhere else, but you can RD anywhere you like. So, why do so many think ED is the best option? Honestly, I am not sure. I have tried to talk many people out of it, yet they persist. The advantage to ED in most people's opinion is that it gives their kid a leg up, so to speak. There is a slightly better likelihood that your child will get accepted with an ED application, but there is also a binding contract to keep you waiting until you hear back. And I've never seen a straightforward answer as to how much more likely acceptance truly is for EDers. A student who decided in September of their senior year of high school rather than by May 1 of their senior year is losing a lot of learning and growth time, too. It's a lot to consider, so I think it must be done on a case-by-case basis.

One of my students, Nicole, applied ED to UNC Chapel Hill, which is a very selective university, so it had a purpose. However, Nicole wasn't exactly sure UNC Chapel Hill was where she wanted to go. It was only the beginning of her senior year (when most kids are applying to college), so she had what she thought was a plan. Then senior year trudged on and friends were chatting: "Where are you going? Did you get into UNC? I got a great offer from Hofstra!" Nicole was thinking, wait, offer? What offer? Colleges do offer financial aid packages with money for good grades or talent. Suddenly the prospect of a one-and-done school selection seemed less inviting. I have seen that scenario happen again and again.

Perhaps Nicole finds the perfect campus (at least according to the virtual tour), plus it's where her best friend is going, plus it's in a warmer climate. Voila! Suddenly the university she EDed to two

90

months ago isn't her top choice anymore, and she's still waiting to hear back. Because now, if Nicole gets in, she has no choice. This scenario alone makes me less inclined to recommend ED, but every case is unique and there are times it works well. Like for my student Meghan, whose parents and grandfather went to Drew University. It was clear she wanted to carry on the legacy, and I didn't blame her. Meghan did apply ED, and she went on to be the third generation in her family to attend Drew.

Quick Crazy Acronym Quiz

Which crazy acronym means to apply to only one school early, but allows you to apply to fourteen more by the regular deadline?

Which crazy acronym allows students to apply early to one school, but requires a guarantee that they will attend should they get accepted?

And . . .

Which crazy acronym means "You lost me four pages ago, and I don't care"?

ELEVEN

The Dangers of the Red Cup . . . and Other Ways to Get Kicked Out of College

Some parents focus so much on getting their kids into college that they rarely consider that there is a possibility that their wonderful bundle-turned-teenager could be thrown out of college. Though it's not very common, it is possible for a student to be expelled and asked to leave the campus for good. There are only a few transgressions that cause enough concern for a college to consider expulsion, so those are the ones I'll talk about. I'm not trying to give you more things to worry about, but I'd hate to see anyone fall victim without at least knowing about the possibility first. Besides, by now I'm sure you know this journey is riddled with minefields; it's better to know where they are ahead of time.

The easiest and likely most common way students can get thrown out of college is drinking alcohol. Students must adhere to the school's rules on alcohol on campus, and those who are underage should understand that they are breaking the law should they choose to drink. According to the most recent statistics from the National Institute on Alcohol Abuse and Alcoholism (NIAAA), it is "estimate[d] that about 1,519 college students ages 18 to 24 die from alcohol-related unintentional injuries, including motor vehicle crashes." Sad, sobering, and largely preventable.

Drinking may seem like an odd topic to cover in a humor book, but I thought it worth mentioning to address the elephant in the room: terrible things parents worry about. It's an extensive list, so I decided to focus on just a couple of sure-fire ways for kids to get in big trouble at college, not every possible way. I'm sure there are some very creative kids out there getting thrown out for all sorts of reasons. Whether or not your kid "goes away" to school, at least some of the multitude of frightening-yet-mostly-ridiculous thoughts running through parents' minds likely include drinking alcohol. Will they drink even though they're not of legal age? (Likely.) Will they remember what I've told them about the dangers of drinking alcohol? (Unlikely.) Perhaps we should scare them out of it. I know, I shouldn't advocate using scare tactics on young adults, because they are still impressionable, but isn't that when you need to do it? At this point parents are running out of time for scare tactics. One last hurrah!

Most of these kids are leaving their homes for the first time to live in a dorm room with other teenagers. Teenagers! Do you recall being a teenager? I know the way my brain worked when I was a teenager. I would never ask my parents what I needed to know. I always trusted the other ill-informed youth I hung out with to get my information, which is dangerous and not very bright. I couldn't even go to the mall alone; I always had my equally inexperienced friends with me. Once my friends and I spent an evening unintentionally talking to a child predator on the phone because we thought she was "funny." Finally, after the crazy woman called like a stalker for two weeks to ask me inappropriate questions with her raspy, male-like voice, my mother caught on and gave her/him an earful. "Donna" never called us anymore after that. Let's face it, teenagers can be clueless.

Ridiculous things seemed like good ideas to us at that age. Drinking beer in quart-size bottles (because it was cheaper that way) and passing the disease-ridden bottle to everyone around for a lovely coagulation of spit, beer, and germs was logical. We also TPed houses simply because we could see them from the woods where we were sitting. I remember joking that they needed "decoration." The teenage brain is not fully formed. Maybe it is close in the physical sense, but the functioning of this organ doesn't really kick in until somewhere around the "terrible twenty-twos," if you're lucky.

Certainly there is peer pressure in middle and high school, but kids don't *live* there. Once they're in college, parents can no longer perform the needed nightly deprogramming necessary to keep their kids' brains functioning with some level of reasoning or at least some fear of repercussions, like grounding or an arrest warrant. Add alcohol to this mess and the parent worry meter blows up.

My sleepless nights led to an attempt at the conversation with my own kids that began with a walk down memory lane:

Remember those insane kids' parties we had where I'd invite forty-six of your closest friends and go to some location that charged an exorbitant amount of money but would allow you all to run around, eat pizza, and scream? Interestingly, those red plastic cups that were always present with your names neatly printed in black Sharpie so you wouldn't randomly drink out of whatever cup was next to you have made their way to college, too. At least that's how it appears on Facebook. These "college cups," let's call them, don't have your name on them this time and are not intended to prevent your catching germs but rather to conceal its contents at every dorm room or frat party.

95

I opted not to tell my kids that I dreamed they were being chased by giant red cups sloshing and spilling over with foamy beer, which I believe was a good call.

I did make sure to tell them not to drink out of any cup but their own, as I'm sure we've all done many times. It was a worry when my kids went off to college with herpes and mono, but now with COVID and its varying mutations, it's another in the long list of what parents will be worrying about. Part of the problem is that kids never really grow up in a parents' eyes; when we look at them, we still see a dirty-faced six-year-old who thought an onion on the counter was an apple and can't understand why his eyes are burning.

We want to believe our kid will make good choices, but man, it's hard sometimes. Parents want to feel confident they won't be getting any calls in the middle of the night from a hospital, EMS worker, or police officer. Not that we wouldn't be awake.

Of course I continued to press my kids as the days grew closer to their departure. I couldn't get the advice out fast enough it seemed; somehow it never struck me as logical to stop giving advice simply because they had never heard any of it. I assumed at least some of it would penetrate. Mostly I talked about what a hangover feels like with blatant hyperbole and descriptive details of vomiting. What good is being a writer if I can't use some sensory detail to scare my children out of drinking?

Sadly, there are other ways to mess up badly at college. In addition to not showing up and/or doing the work that is assigned, the other sure way to get a call from your kids' college or a letter stating their removal is **plagiarism**. Plagiarism doesn't get nearly as much attention as drinking at college does, but in my experience it's a one of the main reasons students have disciplinary issues.

According to plagiarism.org, a survey of about sixty-four thousand US undergrads showed that 36 percent of students admit to "paraphrasing a source" and copying sentences from the Internet, and 38 percent admit "paraphrasing" from a written source. Experts seem to agree on this: No one really knows how common plagiarism is, because it's either undetected or underreported. A study by the Center for Academic Integrity found that almost 80 percent of college students admit to cheating at least once. (I am paraphrasing here, just to be clear.)

As an adjunct professor I teach first-year writing and rhetoric to incoming freshmen at my community college. During my very first semester, one of my students, Don, handed in a draft paper that was clearly not his own work. He'd suddenly gone from disjointed sentences and logical fallacies to writing that sounded like an expert litigator. His first draft was out of sequence and difficult to follow, yet miraculously his next go at it read like a "sample successful essay" from a book about how to write essays. That's because Don's essay was, in fact, a "sample successful essay" from an online source for writing successful essays. It was the *first* example in the article. If you're going to lift your essay from the Internet, at least scroll down to the third or fourth example, Don!

Don didn't stop there, either. He took his "successful" essay example to the Writing Center, presumably to get help with the work he'd stolen. The folks at the Writing Center were not amused. They recommended a failing grade for Don, despite (or because of) his brazenness, I'm still not sure. I ended up giving Don a zero for the draft but allowing him to do one of his own to hand in at the final draft stage. He did so and ultimately passed the course. He also apologized and admitted to the fact that plagiarizing was "a really dumb idea." I'm a bit of softie, but I made clear that it was more than just "dumb." Most colleges take plagiarism very seriously. Many colleges expel students for plagiarizing work. I tell students this at least ten times during the semester, hoping they aren't asleep with their cameras on the cat when I say it.

It's probably not a bad idea to look up a university's policy on plagiarism and share that with your kid at some point before they check out the Olympic-size pool or the renovated food court. Students should know that colleges take plagiarism seriously and that it could result in expulsion. The University of Mississippi reserves the right to revoke a student's degree if they find out said student broke their honor code prior to graduating. Can you imagine having to give back your degree? All because you couldn't remember subject-verb agreement or manage MLA format? The main idea for students is that plagiarism is not worth it. There's too much at stake. Better to hand in a crappy paper than one that makes you a criminal. Students must submit only their own work and words or work that has been properly cited.

Ah, citations, the thorns on the grammar bush that is already a prickly pear. I often work with my students on MLA format before they go to college so they will be ready. If they don't take it seriously, hopefully they will when they get their first poor grade for not citing sources properly. It doesn't usually take more than that, but some kids are stubborn and like to push the envelope. So be sure you have that discussion . . . and stock up on wine and chocolate in case they're ignoring you and focusing on the cat when you do it.

Part of the problem is that most students don't understand what plagiarism is exactly. I believe some end up lifting and copying more out of ignorance and laziness rather than deception, although there are some who love to try their hand at deception, too. Those are the same kids whose parents worry about their needing to get their stomach pumped or getting a call from them requiring bail money. Only you know your kid well enough to decide how much you want to scare them, but make it enough to get them not to do it. Ever. Oh, I know . . . maybe parents should tell their kids how great plagiarizing is; then they definitely won't want to do it.

One more item worth discussing is social media. Kids need to be careful what they post on their social media accounts—yes, all of them. Colleges do look at students' socials and have rescinded acceptances and removed students for certain transgressions. The most common one is hate speech or any racist, misogynistic, inappropriate posts involving the degrading or berating of others.

In 2020 the University of Florida rescinded an acceptance of a student for a racist comment on Instagram. The student's post read: "I really try so hard not to be a racist person, but I most definitely am, there's no denying it." I'm sure that student (nor his or her parents) had any idea that a post like that would mean his plans for college would be derailed, but it is the case more often than people realize.

When I read about these events, I always feel the same way I do when a criminal decides to videotape him- or herself committing a crime: *Why though?!* Maybe because I'm old and had my youth at a time when no one could record it for posterity, but why would anyone want to preserve a bad decision or express a dumb thought to the entire world? This topic is harder to navigate for older parents, but no matter the generation, parents do need to have this important discussion with their kids. Many high schools are having talks about social media and privacy with students as well, which is a good thing. But I remember high school assemblies when I was young; I couldn't tell you what any one of them was about. It was an out-of-class break and opportunity to sit with your friends and giggle about nothing. My kids once had a high school assembly where the principal's pronunciation of the word *peanuts* sounded like *penis* and it became the running joke for the next several weeks. Neither of my kids could tell me what the hell that assembly was about.

Clearly, a serious conversation is needed. I talk with every student I have about this. I would hate for any students to unknowingly post something they think is just their "opinion" and find out later that their opinion just got them kicked out of college. They need to learn early that kind words take you further in life and kind deeds will carry you quicker to whatever destination you choose. If you can get your kid to read this with you, I would say to him or her, as kindly as possible: Don't say mean shit. Don't copy others' words or ideas. Don't drink out of others' cups or break the law. And, please, keep stupid behavior off your socials. In my day, that's what the woods were for.

Special note: For parents who are concerned about alcohol consumption and/or talking with their children about drinking, the NIAAA suggests a combination of individual and environmental interventions for children to maximize positive effects. They say, "Strong leadership from a concerned college president in combination with engaged parents, an involved campus community, and a comprehensive program of evidence-based strategies can help address harmful student drinking." Or you can talk to the college's **provost**; no one knows what that person does anyway, so might as well put him or her to work!

If you or someone you know needs help, visit:

https://www.collegedrinkingprevention.gov/CollegeAIM for more information.

TWELVE

Grade A (or B or C . . .)

One of my least favorite parts of being an educator is grading. As a private tutor, I opt not to grade and rely instead on feedback, reflection, and discussion. However, students do not have such an option in school. Grades are a measuring stick to determine how students are doing, what they are (or aren't) learning, and their skill level. These days students have little to no way of hiding or changing those grades before parents can look at them. With software that allows students and their parents constant access to grades, many are checking their grades online regularly (read: obsessively). It's unhealthy, and not in a good way, like french fries.

Grades are a conundrum: a necessary guide to be sure students obtain the education they need and an obstacle to getting into college if they don't measure up. Because of this pressure, I know many parents (me) who have stormed into a school building to contest their kid's grades more than once. I recall when my son was in middle school and missed the honor roll because he failed gym. How does one fail gym? Well, in Ryan's case he forgot his sneakers and gym clothes at least once a week. I love my kid more than pizza, but he is not good at the minutia of life.

When I realized that this infraction was the *only* reason he could not be on the honor roll, the mom spikes erupted up my back. Once again, I put on my cape and went into Super Mom mode—protector and perfector of the flakey behavior of her children. I argued with the principal, a very patient man, that Ryan still participated actively in gym, despite his mindlessness when leaving the house. He had no prior disciplinary issues (he was ten). I felt like a defense attorney for a client who just videotaped himself stealing a box of Twinkies by eating them in the store from which he stole them. Ryan is a brilliant mind and a kind heart, but he forgot his lunch so often when he was young that dropping his brown bag at school on my way to work became the first leg of my commute.

I can't help but wonder, though, *What if I had backed off?* Realizing now that honor roll for one marking period in the fifth grade means essentially nothing, I wish I had had (yet another) talk with him about responsibility. Maybe the 467th conversation about leaving the milk on the counter would have stuck. We will never know.

Perhaps allowing kids to "get it wrong" sometimes is a necessary element for getting it right. Ryan still occasionally struggles with scattered brain (and messy hair), but he can pull it together, something he learned to do in college, where Super Mom (and most definitely her cape) were not allowed. Kids need to learn the skills of navigation. I have noticed that parents tend to "drive" the college process, which leaves their kids in the back seat, likely doom scrolling the low acceptance rates of all their favorite colleges. How can parents begin to hand over the reins before their scattered young adults leave for a campus where they'll need a map to find the cafeteria?

When kids get to college, they must do things like fill out a **FERPA** form. There's more on FERPA in the Glossary, but basically FERPA gives students who are eighteen the power to decide who gets to see their education records—even for their parents. Yep, you read that correctly: Your child must give permission for you to view their grades. It's an upside-down world where parents pay exorbitant amounts of money so their children can decorate their dorm rooms with lavish bedding, kitchen appliances, and Christmas lights; attend an expensive higher ed program; study in other countries; attend parties; join clubs; and make friends, *and* they get to decide whether their parents can be informed that they're flunking the Principles of Economics. It sort of feels like one of those dystopian teenage novels and leaves parents wondering what the hell happened to the days when grades came home on small cardboard sheets that looked like library cards graded in ink by the hand of a teacher who knew if she used erasable markers parents would never see the correct grade.

Yet here we are—all of us, part of the fun-filled, wallet-draining, eye-rolling event that is prepping for and getting our kids to college. Are we having fun yet? Nothing but the best for our fragile offspring. Don't get me wrong, I love the level of empathy of this generation, as well as their near-universal desire to rid this world of hurtful behavior toward the marginalized; however, many of them missed roll call when the grit and tenacity was being doled out. Maybe they were in gymnastics or had a baseball game that day. It's also likely I was supposed to bring the sliced oranges, set up the snack station, and manage the phone chain that day, but I forgot. I was never good at remembering the cupcakes or other peanut-free snack I was supposed to bring to school.

Many students I have worked with are essentially paralyzed by challenge and failure. Most are simply not equipped for it. I'm not sure if it's due to the "everyone gets a trophy" approach to inclusion or if so many parents were perpetual dragon slayers (as I was), swooping in to breathe fire on any small problem their children encountered. We meant well. How were we supposed to know that our concern and help would lead to a generation of citizens who don't know where to place a stamp or how to clean their cup when the dishwasher breaks? (Yep, another real example.)

Now we want this same group to face challenges head-on and recover quickly from their F in chemistry, or, better yet, not fail the test at all. How can parents help without saving?

Well, grades can be a good place to start. Students are given many chances, sometimes pushed by parents, coached by guidance counselors, and encouraged by school psychologists, and still they procrastinate. What if the F they "earned" on their literature exam was indicative of exactly how much effort they put into it? As parents we can't hold an intervention each time our kids screw up. Sometimes maybe they need to get the F. The sooner this is done, the easier and less complicated it is. I should have let Ryan's gym teacher give him the grade he deserved. Even if I secretly (well, not so secretly I guess) think it's a stupid policy. The disappointment Ryan would likely have felt may have been the lesson that he desperately needed. And the experience might have resulted in my not having to drop his forgotten lunch five times a week. Or maybe he would not have cared less, which was, for me, even more terrifying.

When kids get to college, they must figure out each class, each professor, and each assignment without their parents, tutors, coaches, guidance counselors, custodians, or anyone else. It takes time and is a struggle for some, because it's unfamiliar territory. But that is exactly what college is about: the unfamiliar. Sometimes, when left to their own choices and consequences, kids learn lessons. They might fail first though (possibly even several times).

One of my students, Guy, was struggling with Spanish in his junior year—you know, the *big* year for grades. Guy knew exactly what he wanted to study in college and what kind of career he was interested in; he was one of those rare students who had it all planned out. However, he was struggling in Spanish and hated the class. Guy and his parents were at their wit's end because he still had another year to go and any more of this language instruction was going to negatively affect his GPA.

We discussed possibilities: switching to a different language, getting a tutor, doing extra credit. But I recommended something more radical. I asked, "What if Guy just doesn't take a language next year?"

Grades serve as signposts, too. We checked the colleges that Guy was applying to and most of them required three years of a language, not four. Others didn't specify and indicated that language classes can be taken at their college if not done before, which makes sense if you remember that universities are businesses. "Oh, you need some extra classes? Sure thing!" It would cost his parents more to do it that way, but they were able and more than willing just to end the madness of Spanish homework sheets with conjugated verbs and words with their own gender.

Regardless of how it would play out for Guy, he realized he had options and failing Spanish would likely not mark the end of all his hopes and dreams; though it might make it harder to impress the cute classmate from Spain he just met and wanted to communicate with. Or perhaps Guy would take Spanish the next semester, just so she could tutor him. The possibilities are endless if Guy is presented with his options and does the deciding. It means he will also be learning from each choice he makes. It's possible he will take a Spanish course in college, do well, and the girl will still leave him halfway through the semester.

I, myself, approach school like a puzzle. Each teacher is a different piece, and when you figure out where that piece fits into your puzzle, it's a lot easier to manage his or her assignments and expectations. It's not always about working harder, even in college. Sometimes it's about working smarter. When I was in college, back when the dinosaurs roamed, I had this teacher who loved Herman Melville. I was not much of a Melville fan; I thought he was a privileged scholar who was born into money and became famous because of that privilege. Unlike my hero, Willy Shakespeare, who wrote his plays and poems mostly at the local pub. That's my kind of guy.

As I faced *Moby Dick*'s four-hundred-plus pages of unabridged horror, I realized I needed to find out why this professor loved this author so much, or at least be able to find something about the guy I could vibe with. Finding a common denominator with the professor puts you on solid ground and in a better position for fawning, if needed. Now, as a teacher, I understand that most educators want their students to see what they see in a hypothesis or an example or an exceptionally long and arduous work of literature. There was something about this classic my professor felt was worth teaching. As a student, my job was to find it. I didn't have to agree with her necessarily, but I had to at least take it in as best I could to form an opinion of my own, an educated one, based on my own thoughts about *Moby Dick*, other than, *Wow, this is one really angry whale.*

As it turned out, my professor was right about Melville as a writer. *Moby Dick* was an incredible romp through man versus nature, power versus respect, and fate versus free will. Unexpectedly, it spoke to me in ways no other book ever had. Whether or not we create our own fates became a great philosophical exploration for me. At least for a day or two.

For students, grades come through exploration and a willingness to be open and do the work. Their responsibility is to show up, pay attention, and give each class their best shot. Hopefully, along the way through college, they unexpectedly learn something cool or wonderful. Or at least they figure out where to put the stamp on the envelope.

So to recap . . .

- Grades are necessary and a little stupid at the same time.

- Most kids today do not know how to address and stamp an envelope or wash dishes by hand.

- Maybe let your kid fail, a little. When we were young, our parents let us fail and just made fun of us after, and it worked out okay (unless you ask my therapist, I suppose).

- FERPA is ridiculous; don't give your kid that much power.

- *Moby Dick* really is a fabulous book, but I'm not sure a story about a mad mammal needed to be quite that long.

THIRTEEN

Dorm Days

In my opinion, which by now you're probably quite accustomed to, one of the best parts of the college experience for parents is move-in day. Yes, it's emotional and a bit sad, but overall, it's a Blue Ribbon Day for parents. You did it! You succeeded at getting your kid to college or whatever next step they have arrived at—it doesn't matter, they're off your couch! Yet, for the unprepared, this day, too, has the potential to devolve into a *Brady Bunch* episode where the dog knocks over the catering table and Marcia needs a nose job. Oh, Marcia, Marcia, Marcia!

Preparation can be—hell, I know it sucks to have to always be preparing for something, but it *is* helpful. Plan a strategy and logistics for the day they move in, but leave open the rest. It's an emotionally charged event, so setting expectations can leave everyone involved spent and disappointed before you even arrive at the dormitory.

Many kids and parents cry, but not all do, so don't think your kid is an uncaring sociopath if he or she shows absolutely no emotion. Likewise, if your kid is a blubbering fool (or you are), don't worry too much. It's not indicative of what the next four years will be—hopefully.

For my own son, leaving home turned out to be harder than he had imagined. Two years before senior year, Ryan wanted to attend school in Australia. Yes, that Australia. Across the world! I knew I shouldn't have bought him that stupid globe. I imagine he wanted to go for no logical reason other than to get far away from his suburban bubble and experience life on his own (because it couldn't be to get away from me). Ryan was more emotional than I think even he expected. Leaving is hard for most of them, even when they say otherwise. Every young person wants an adult's life—until they have it and realize it was all a terrible trick and being young really is *way* better. This is the age-old wisdom that still has not been able to transfer to the next generation before it's too late.

So many kids continue to believe it's better over here in adult world, but we know it's not. Others do seem to understand the magnitude of the life change they are experiencing, but they leave anyway, and their parents don't sleep for four years. When I asked Jess at the beginning of her senior year of high school if she was ready for college, I wasn't being snarky at all, which is quite shocking because I enjoy a good snark. It just seemed to me that students are asked to move along, expected to follow someone else's timetable. That doesn't suit a lot of kids, and it was a challenge for Jess. She only had one year to prepare, but teenager life is like dog years—a lot happens in a year, and they can grow up more than you might think. Or they can continue to hoard forks in their room and lose their car keys.

Jess found a way, as many students do, to face her fears and realize this experience was mostly paid for by someone else or with borrowed money. It seemed less like reality, and she could ignore the parts that overwhelmed her, at least for a while. And *that* is what teenagers are made for. They have been training their entire lives to ignore the important! What better way to exercise their skill but on the most expensive, important thing they have had in their lives thus far: a college education. Therefore, my hair is a frizzy mess and gray in patches and has streaks on the sides that make me look like an aging Morticia Adams in the morning—before coffee—and in serious need of a spa day.

When you arrive at "move-in day," "drop-off day," or whatever cheeky slogan the university gives it where you are going, you will be told exactly where to go and what to do. The universities are very good at this and usually even hand you a map. Most colleges make it a mostly structured event, which leaves me wondering if that's for the student or to keep the parents in line. Maybe both. If you've never seen a parent standing on a college campus after his or her kid is scurried away by some staff member with a name tag and wearing the school's colors—it's a pathetic site. I looked like a UFO had just dropped me there; I had absolutely no idea where I was or what to do. It's like the Oscar winners after their speeches on stage. They always look around for the person who is going to tell them where to go. I guess it must be so they don't look stupid scurrying around the stage in an overpriced, hard-to-manage evening gown. But they've seen it done a million times; how do they not know this by now? If you came from the left, you go right, and vice versa. Man, someone should give me an Oscar, I'd know how to do it.

But I get it—nervousness can take over and suddenly you're flattening the grass because you're walking back and forth fifty times trying to drop your kid off at college and go home. That's what happens to many parents on drop-off day; the emotion and stress of the moment, the elation, as well as the fear, surround them and create a buzz in the brain that makes them look like deer in the headlights of a Ford F-150, except they're wearing a sweatshirt that says "University of Tampa."

I remember standing on the curb at Hofstra University for nearly twenty minutes, sort of paralyzed in place after Ryan had been whisked away and it was time for me to go home. Alone this time. I was no better when Jess had left two years prior. I walked in circles to the car and then back, thinking of something else I wanted to say. Then I decided what I was going to say was stupid, and I needed to leave her alone and walk back to the car again. I was recalculating like a GPS stuck on a loop. It would have been frightening if not for the several other malfunctioning guardians wandering around the parking lot with me.

The colleges do offer a good deal of preparation to try to avoid this sad scene, but it never seems like enough for some of us. Students attend lengthy orientations, and parents connect with other parents to make Facebook pages and volunteer lists. I can't believe that I was still on a volunteer list and my kids were away at college. There is always a shortage of phone chain workers it seems. Haven't parents paid enough dues by then? All the ticket and booster sales; bake sales; fundraisers; and gluten-free, nut-free, sugar-free shitty birthday cupcakes, and it's still not enough? I started to think I would probably end up creating a houseware drive for my kids' pots and dishes too—should they ever actually leave for good.

Universities are actually extremely helpful in this regard. They present tired parents with offers for dorm refrigerators, XL sheets (for the college's longer twin beds so you can't buy regular sheets on sale), and laundry service before your kid even graduates high school. We know it's a ploy to sell us more crap . . . frankly, we don't care. We're tired. And if I had to drive up there and back again before my kid's first class, I would have certainly been angry-driving and well positioned for a ticket on the highway. It's amazing how quickly you can go from "I miss my kid" to "I am *not* driving up there again this month!"

Colleges know that by move-in time, parents are about as spent as all their money. So we take our broke asses home and order everything but a kitchen sink for our kids, mostly to make them happy, but also so they won't bother us.

Once you have prepared for the sad or long goodbye, let it go. Try to enjoy this amazing day. Take your kids' lead. Do they want you to stay and help make the bed, or would they rather do it themselves? Some kids find it difficult to say goodbye and don't want to have an ugly cry in front of their new roommate, who they met just six minutes ago. Try not to be insulted if they need some time alone. Chances are they will call you or come home at the first opportunity, with their mountain of laundry and expensive sheets they haven't washed once all semester.

Parents should consider planning something else for when they arrive home. It doesn't have to be anything but a cup of tea and a bath or a glass of wine and reruns of *Frasier*, it doesn't matter. Somehow knowing you planned to do something, on your own, after they are gone, makes it less depressing. Well, that and maybe stopping on your way home for some ice cream.

If all that fails, trust me when I say you will be back to move them again before you know it. It's so exciting the first time you move them in, but the next year and the one after that and the one after that become less exciting and more like you have a friend who you've help move eight times, and they don't even send you a Christmas card. Moving kids in and then out and then in and out again . . . you will be so sick of squeezing that stupid oversize Sponge Bob pillow into the car and hanging Christmas lights over their bed and cleaning out refrigerators that each drive home will get progressively less depressing. You might even look forward to whatever you planned for when you get home. Ben, Jerry, I'm on my way!

What the hell do I do now?

- Your kid is in college, drink wine! When you get home, though, not on the road.

- Don't cry for too long; before you know it, it will be time to move them out again.

- Your car will never be big enough for this, especially if you have a daughter, so consider the U-Haul thing or make friends with someone who owns a truck.

- Celebrate a little; you have managed to get through this ridiculous mouse maze and reached the end—drink more wine!

- Call your friends; they're drinking wine too!

FOURTEEN

Giving Advice . . . to a Kid
Who Doesn't Want Any Advice

Because Jess is my oldest, I began worrying about college when she was a junior in high school. I was fortunate; most parents these days begin worrying before their kid is even in high school. For me, it seemed the present moment and everything ahead of it had become simply terrifying to consider. My near-incessant chatter about what she needed to know was like a semiautomatic weapon firing off item after item at her in quick succession. Jess also didn't seem to appreciate my barging into her room at two in the morning with some new and emphatic warning about some such danger she had not encountered yet, but likely would. Her groggy face and bed head hair did not deter me, but her begging me to go back to bed was fair, I suppose. So, instead, I began writing down the items I worried about.

Not to toot my own horn, but I am an excellent worrier, an over-achiever of obsession. I worried about Jess going out when she got to college—alone or with strange people I didn't know. Simultaneously, I was also afraid she'd never go anywhere. I worried about her grades, and the professors who would give her a hard time when I wasn't there to go complain to the principal. They don't have principals at college, and, as I said, no one knows what the hell a "provost" does. (I did solve this mystery eventually; head to the Glossary to find out what a provost is.)

I worried whether she'd do her homework and assignments as and when instructed, or forget and then when I reminded her, she'd say, "I'm working on it!" which always meant *no, I haven't even looked at it.* What would happen when I was no longer there for her to lie to while she was procrastinating?!

What if Jess couldn't find her classrooms or the buildings where her classes were? Maybe a young, kind professor would help her. There must be some. But then I'd worry that she'd fall in love with said young, kind professor, who just so happened to be a young, kind, *married* professor, but she loved him with wild abandon because he loved her writing and saw straight through to her soul! That's about where Jess would ask me to leave her room and tell me to stop the madness.

And I tried. Often. Yet the worry would return like a many headed hydra; each moment was another evil skull to wrack mine with fear. On the days when I could imagine her away at school with friends and sitting on student furniture, only comfortable to the young, and laughing and happy, then those thoughts would immediately be followed by a worry about college parties. What if someone dropped ecstasy into her drink? What if she decided to **pledge** a sorority? Do sororities do **hazing**, or is that just fraternities?

I wondered if she'd know not to do laundry at night if it was in some creepy basement area of the dormitory building. Jess liked to be alone often, so when I wasn't worried about parties, I would obsess

116

over the thoughts of her roaming campus on her own, encountering seedy people and criminal activity. I never saw any seedy people nor any criminal activity on her campus or any we visited, but I was sure they were there, lurking in the shadows of the student bookstore. My sister-in-law and I bought her protective equipment such as mace spray and a loud air horn. We're Sicilian, so paranoia is a family experience. Distrust, superstition, and worry are basically woven into our DNA. So I worried Jess would simply throw the protective equipment into a drawer and forget about them until a drunk friend in her room decided to try the mace out as breath spray or hit the air horn and wake up the entire dorm floor, resulting in disciplinary action.

The "what ifs" were endless. *What if she walked into town and then got lost, unable to find her way back until dark—and without the protective equipment her aunt and I so diligently supplied? What if she got amnesia and . . .* The worry list seemed more like a tirade of unwelcome thoughts, unless I drank enough wine. Then I couldn't hold a coherent thought for more than four seconds, which seemed like a good idea initially, but then drinking never worked out either, because the worry didn't stop there—drunk Linda graduated to nonsensical worries. I bet I know what you are thinking: *Wasn't she already there?* Apparently, no, I was not.

The nonsensical worry goes deeper into one worry world instead of scattering its energy to many topics—a worry wormhole, if you will. Once I enter the dark worry wormhole, I have sudden, stark, and, well, stupid thoughts. I thought perhaps Jess would become so homesick and need me, and I wouldn't get there fast enough. Then I recalled her overnight trip to a music camp in sixth grade, when she procrastinated and doubted her decision to go. I thought I was being a responsible parent telling her to "follow through with her commitments" and "take responsibility for the things she signs up for" as well as other worn-out clichés intended to motivate her but mostly just annoyed her. I cajoled and convinced and was feeling a touch of

"Mother of the Year" the moment she decided to finish packing and head out. My temporary hubris ended abruptly, though, when the call came. The camp counselor said she wanted me to know because Jess said it was her *first* period ever, but that she was fine and resting comfortably. I had sent my eleven-year-old off to play clarinet at a band camp where she knew not one soul, where she did not want to go, and . . . she got her period for the first time—without me there. "I'm fine, Mom," slid through the phone, but what I heard was, "I needed you; where were you, Mom?" To which my mind added, *I survived the embarrassment, but just barely . . . I felt so alone. You're the worst mom ever.*

I feared sending her off to a college in another state could only be a worse debacle. The descent down the wormhole continued as my mind played the reel of all the moments I had failed to prepare her for: *Did she know where to go if she got sick? Did I show her how to contact campus security? Would she remember to sign up for classes early before all the "good" professors' classes were filled?* As I thought of these, and was denied any further access to her room, I began writing them down. I decided I was going to keep going until I exhausted myself of terrible scenarios. *There has to be an end to it*, I thought. I wrote and wrote, as though each idea written seeded yet another worry to grow the list, and I could not offer her the advice my worry brain wanted to impart. Mostly because she wouldn't let me.

Eventually, though, I got tired, not only in the wrist from scribbling ferociously, but also my mind was tired. I think I heard my brain finally say, *Please . . stop . . . seriously.* Or maybe it was Jess texting me back when I frantically texted three times in a row to see if she was okay, and she was only in her room packing. Either way, Jess did need me, but not in the way I was thinking or was used to. She needed me to hold it together and give her measured advice, not frantic ramblings.

So I took my ramblings to the page, and eventually they became a hardcover book I made for her before she left for college. It was my *Book of Advice* . . . for my daughter who didn't want any advice. I put all my worry into sections so she could easily look up topics that she may encounter while she was away. I'm not sure if she ever used it, but she did say she read it. I didn't quiz her on that, because I figured if she was lying about reading it, that was still kind of nice. She would at least score points for kindness.

For me, though, the gift encapsulated my worries into one place. A place that I could close and give to her. I could feel as though I had told her all the things I wanted to, even if I didn't. I put all I had for her into that book, and it allowed me to give it to her ceremoniously and symbolically. She was eighteen at this point, so it's quite likely she didn't read it or understand its purpose, but I figured, well at least I could morph the worry into some semblance of useful advice, and she would know how much I love her.

I knew I was on to something, too, because at Jess's college drop-off, I cried and made her bed, and cried more and hung up her clothes, and cried again, and then hung around until it was dark while crying. Ryan was totally patient and quiet during this solemn event. I left only begrudgingly with more tears, but then, on the car ride home, Ryan asked me, "So, are you gonna write a book like that for *me* when I go to college, too?"

"Well, yes, yes indeed I am."

I found ways to help myself through this process and you will too. It's a crazy ride that travels through many emotional twists and turns along the way. Follow your heart . . . because your head will make you nutty. Also, don't forget to pat yourself on the back occasionally. Your child is growing up and planning his or her future. Yay! No matter how much confusion or ambivalence your kid might experience, and no matter how slow the pace, he or she is trudging ahead, moving forward. And *that* is something to be proud of.

Glossary of Some Common College Terms

(mostly to impress your friends)

529 Plan: A US tax-advantage savings account designed for flexible use in paying educational expenses. You can save on taxes while saving for college.

Common Application: (also called Common App) an undergraduate college admissions application platform containing nearly nine hundred higher education institutions across the United States and twenty other countries.

The Common App allows users to apply to many colleges with the same information and organize and list information.

Conservatories: Colleges for the study of classical music, performing arts, and other studies in the arts. Often conservatories are considered separate divisions within the university.

Courses and programs are based in practical training and offer frequent opportunities for students to perform.

FERPA form: FERPA stands for Family Educational Rights and Privacy Act. Passed by Congress in 1974, this act grants specific rights to students concerning their educational records. These rights begin as soon as students enroll or registers with an academic program of a university.

In basic terms, a student's education records are confidential and may not be released by any staff member of the university without written consent of the student. Faculty has a responsibility to protect education records in their possession from being released, even to parents. Filling out the FERPA form can grant parents the right to view their child's grades and other information.

Ivy League: The Ivy League is a group of established colleges and universities in the northeastern United States with a high academic and social prestige. This group includes the following colleges: Harvard, Yale, Princeton, Columbia, Dartmouth, Cornell, Brown, and the University of Pennsylvania.

Hazing: Difficult, strenuous, often humiliating, sometimes dangerous tasks performed as initiation for college students seeking membership to a fraternity or sorority.

Hundreds of years old, hazing is a process that can include acts involving alcohol and/or physical injury, assault, kidnapping and other frightening or illegal acts.

Plagiarism: The act of adopting and using another person's words or ideas as one's own without giving credit to the originator or using proper citation.

According to Merriam-Webster: "If schools wish to impress upon their students how serious an offense plagiarism is, they might start with an explanation of the word's history. *Plagiarize* (and *plagiarism*) comes from the Latin *plagiarius* [meaning] 'kidnapper.'"

Pledging: A promise or agreement to join a fraternity, sorority, or secret society.

Pledging involves different mandatory activities and meetings, often requiring a large commitment of time and effort. New members spend a lot of time learning about the different aspects of their fraternity or sorority.

Provost: A high-ranking university administrative official. (Well, that clears it up.)

Because that definition is vague and useless, the easier path is to compare the role to the position of dean at a college or university. A dean oversees an institution's faculty and academic staff at the departmental level, while a provost oversees an institution's entire educational offering. A dean's main responsibility is to ensure that departments meet their academic goals, while a provost's main responsibility is to oversee the overall development of all the educational programs that a college or university offers.

For the maddening acronyms ED, EA, RD, and SCEA, see the sidebar box in the section "To ED or Not to ED" for a full description.

Acknowledgments

For my mother,
Thanks for the funny.
For my father,
I could have done nothing without your love and encouragement.

For my children, Jess and Ryan, there is no book without you--somewhat because half the stories in this book are about you! But more because parenting you both, I have learned as much as I have taught. Your creative spirits are like a guiding force, and our bond of three, forever tethered, lights the way for our creative pursuits and warms us with the feeling of home.

For my partner, thank you for standing by my side through this crazy thing called life. Thanks for not reacting when I would awake at all hours to write something or have to do "research" while on vacation. You're a great wingman. I love you.

For the "Maries," my writer's group and sisters of my heart; thank you for the endless meets and imposter syndrone conversations. For seeing my procrastination and raising me one senior moment, I love you both.

For my brother, Pat, and sis, Georgette, thank you for never being sick of hearing about "the book" and being endlessly encouraging.

For my friends and colleauges, without whom nothing gets accomplished, thank you for listening, reading (repeatedly), and encouraging me on this journey.

To my VCFA cohort, I am indebted to you for your support and kindness. To Patrick Madden, and the other stellar teachers, advisors, administrators of VCFA, there is no book without you either. More importantly, there is no writer. Thank you for continually propping me back up and reminding me who I am.

Thank you Woodhall Press for giving me a chance and leading without taking over. I'm so thrilled we connected.

For my students, you know I joke about your generation sometimes... because it's funny! But I love each of you and appreciate your fun, sometimes silly, sometimes heart breaking, struggles and triumphs. Thanks for letting me be part of your life at a challenging yet important time. Go do great things!

For parents, I see you. I've been you. I thank you, and I am grateful that you've allowed me to walk with you along this crazy road. Let's meet up for wine!

About the Author

A professional content specialist for over 20 years, Linda Presto has worked in corporate communications, advertising, and magazine and newspaper publishing. Linda has been an English and Writing tutor for over 20 years and is a writer who coaches students preparing for college and beyond. Her business, College Coaching with Care, includes expertise in SAT/ACT prep, college and scholarship searches, applications, essays, resumes, interview preparation, personal statements, strategy, as well as school and career planning. Linda lives in New Jersey with her family.